# Integrative Counselling Primer

Richard Worsley

***PCCS BOOKS***
Monmouth

First published 2007

PCCS Books Ltd
Wyastone Business Park
Wyastone Leys
Monmouth
NP25 3SR
UK
Tel +44 (0)1600 891 509
www.pccs-books.co.uk



**The Integrative Counselling Primer**

A CIP catalogue record for this book is available from the British Library

ISBN 978 1 898059 81 3

*Cover design by Old Dog Graphics*
*Printed in the UK by Severn, Gloucester*

# CONTENTS


| | | |
|---|---|---|
| INTRODUCTION | | 1 |
| Chapter 1 | INTEGRATION THE PERSON-CENTRED WAY | 6 |
| Chapter 2 | SOME PERSON-CENTRED PRINCIPLES | 19 |
| Chapter 3 | INTEGRATING NEW THINKING IN PERSON-CENTRED THEORY: CONFIGURATIONS OF SELF | 31 |
| Chapter 4 | THE SPACE BETWEEN PEOPLE: EGO-STATE THEORY | 41 |
| Chapter 5 | EMBODIED AWARENESS: THE MIND'S MIRROR | 52 |
| Chapter 6 | COUNSELLING AS DIALOGUE: WORKING WITH MEANING IN THERAPY | 61 |
| Chapter 7 | AN INTEGRATIVE COUNSELLING TRANSCRIPT | 74 |
| Chapter 8 | SMALL-SCALE PRACTITIONER RESEARCH | 83 |
| Chapter 9 | INTEGRATING THE SELF: A CONCLUSION | 91 |
| Appendix | RESOURCES FOR LEARNING | 103 |
| GLOSSARY | | 106 |
| REFERENCES | | 114 |
| INDEX | | 119 |

**DEDICATION**

For Maggie Taylor-Sanders, who helped me to see what I think through other eyes, and for Mary Virginia Baird Vivian, a warm friend and fine counsellor.

# SERIES INTRODUCTION

PETE SANDERS

## COUNSELLING

Before we launch into exploring an integrative way of working, it might be helpful to take a look at some definitions of counselling itself. It is important to locate the helping activity of counselling in relation to other helping activities in order to avoid confusion regarding the purpose of this book. This book is specifically aimed at people wanting to learn about integrative counselling with no previous experience or knowledge of counselling or psychology. The key word here is counselling.

So what do we mean by counselling?

### What is counselling for?

One way of defining counselling is to look at what it is useful for. In the past thirty years, counselling has become ubiquitous, and it is perilously close to being presented as a panacea for just about everything. Some critics say that the emerging 'profession' of counselling has much to gain for claiming, on behalf of counsellors and therapists, that counselling is good for everything. It would be wrong to make such claims: counselling has its limits and part of being a counsellor is to know what those limits are. The problem is that when we are in distress, it is comforting to think that there is a simple answer around the corner.

The situation is not made any easier when we understand that simply sitting down and taking time out from a busy life can make things seem better. Counsellors must be able to explain to their clients the differences between this very important relief and comfort that can be gained from compassionate human contact on the one hand, and counselling as a specialist activity on the other. Counselling can help people in certain states of distress and usually involves change:

- change in the way the client sees things or themselves
- change in the way a client thinks about things or themselves
- change in the way a client feels about things or themselves
- change in the way a client behaves

Although many people will not be able to put it neatly into a few words, what they seek from counselling can be roughly summarised in a few categories:

- support
- recovery
- problem-solving
- gaining insight or self-awareness
- developing new strategies for living

The sort of distress that counselling can help is often called 'emotional' or 'psychological' and can include:

- stress—a very general and possibly over-used term, but there are some situations in life, especially those that you can't control, that might leave you feeling so stressed that it interferes with your everyday life
- conflict—at home or work
- bereavement—whether a relative or friend. Indeed, having anything permanently taken away might lead to a feeling of bereavement, such as losing your job or losing your ability to do something like walk, play sport or have sex
- depression—another over-used term and not one to be taken lightly. Many life events can make us feel low, and talking it over really does help. The popular term 'depression' can cover everything from feeling understandably low after having your purse stolen or losing your job, through to being unable to get up in the morning or eat properly because you think life is not worth living
- coping with poor health, e.g. having a long-standing health problem or receiving a diagnosis of a serious or terminal illness

- trauma, e.g. surviving (including witnessing) something very disturbing (including abuse of various forms)

**What counselling is not for**

When someone decides to attend counselling sessions, they are, by definition, distressed. It is, therefore, particularly important that the client doesn't have either their time wasted or their distress increased by attending something that we might reasonably predict would be of no help.

As we have already seen, it is difficult to honestly predict whether counselling will definitely help in a particular circumstance. Nevertheless there are times when counselling is clearly not the first or only appropriate INTERVENTION. It is doubly difficult to appear to turn someone away when they arrive because sometimes:

- part of their distress might be that they have difficulty feeling understood and valued
- they may lack self-confidence and a rejection would damage it even more
- they have been to other types of helper and they think that counselling is their last hope
- they are so desperate they might consider suicide

However difficult it might be, we have to be completely honest with clients if we think counselling is not going to help. It would be wrong to let them find out after a number of sessions, after which they might feel that they are to blame for not trying hard enough. The use of counselling should be questioned if it is likely that their symptoms of distress are caused by:

- poor housing or homelessness
- poverty
- lack of opportunity due to discrimination or oppression

Problems of this nature are best addressed by social action. The counsellor as a citizen shares responsibility with all other members of society to remove these blocks to peoples' physical and psychological well-being.

It would be convenient if we could divide problems up into

two neat categories; those of psychological origin (and amenable to counselling) and those of non-psychological origin (and therefore not amenable to counselling). However, there are some other causes of distress which, although they will not be *solved* by counselling, will undoubtedly be helped by counselling in that the person concerned will be able to function better with the kind of support that counselling can provide. It may also be that the client experiences repetitive patterns of self-defeating thoughts and behaviour which renders them less effective in dealing with problems which do not have a psychological origin. It might also be that a person would be better able to challenge an oppressive system if they felt personally empowered, and counselling can sometimes achieve this. Such problems include those caused by:

- poor health (a physical illness or ORGANIC CONDITION)
- oppression and discrimination, including bullying
- living in an abusive relationship

Counsellors must be constantly vigilant to ensure that their work with a particular client, or clients in general, is not contributing to disadvantage, abuse and oppression by rendering people more acceptant of poor conditions, whether at work or at home.

> Psychologists must join with persons who reject racism, sexism, colonialism and exploitation and must find ways to redistribute social power and to increase social justice. PRIMARY PREVENTION RESEARCH inevitably will make clear the relationship between social pathology and PSYCHOPATHOLOGY and then will work to change social and political structures in the interests of social justice. It is as simple and as difficult as that! (Albee, 1996: 1131, cited in Davies & Burdett, 2004: 279)

## What is 'personal growth'?

Counselling in the UK has become associated with what might be called the 'personal growth industry'. Self-improvement has been a feature of our society for a hundred years or more and includes such initiatives as the Workers' Education Association supporting the educational needs of working men and women. More recently, further education has embraced more nonvocational courses and reflects the fact that as we get more affluent we have to attend less to the business of mere survival. We can turn our attention to getting more out of life and along with other self-development activities, improving our psychological well-being proves to be a popular choice. Furthermore, when people have a good experience as a client, they sometimes see that learning to be a counsellor could be a further step in self-improvement.

This 'personal growth' use of counselling contrasts with counselling as a treatment for more acute forms of psychological distress as listed on pages 2 and 3 above. It is, however, no less worthy or ultimately useful. Fulfilled, happy citizens, able to put good helping skills back into their communities are an asset, not a handicap.

## Using the glossary

You may have noticed that some words are set in SMALL CAPITALS. This indicates that the glossary on page 106 carries a brief definition and explanation of the term. The SMALL CAPITALS can appear anywhere in the texts, quotes, subtitles or index.

# 1

# INTEGRATION
# THE PERSON-CENTRED WAY

> Therapists must convey to the patient that their paramount task is to build a relationship together that will itself become the agent of change ... Above all, the therapist must be prepared to go wherever the patient goes, do all that is necessary to continue building trust and safety in the relationship. I try to tailor the therapy for each patient, to find the best way to work. (Yalom, 2001: 34–5)

This book describes a way of being with the client in counselling which is *both* PERSON-CENTRED *and* INTEGRATIVE. It is a subtly different approach to CLASSICAL CLIENT-CENTRED COUNSELLING (CCCC). The heart of CCCC is also the heart of this approach. (It is useful, but not essential for the reader already to have read Pete Sanders' (2006) *The Person-Centred Counselling Primer*.)

This book will help the reader consider how to derive useful understanding from other theories of counselling, while remaining person-centred. It will help the reader see why being rooted in person-centredness is so important. It will link the integration of theory to personal integration, the growth of the counsellor as a whole person. Above all, it will stress the need to be fully present to clients, to be real. Therefore, I want to begin the journey with the word IDIOSYNCRATIC.

IDIOSYNCRATIC certainly does not mean odd or quirky in a derogatory sense. Rather, it means that the therapy is about as far away from formulas and conformity as possible. The therapist attempts to bring all of herself to bear in relating to the whole of the client. In his later years, Carl Rogers became very irritated with the commonly held view that person-centred therapy was just a matter of reflecting feelings or parroting back to the client the words they used (Rogers, 1986). A mechanistic reflection of feeling is a poor portrayal of empathy. Clients will quickly sense the difference between a therapist being genuine and one just going through the motions. Therapy must feel alive. It is a considered and yet spontaneous response to the client, in which the therapist engages in a DIALOGUE of real human depth. To paraphrase the chapter title from which Yalom's words, above, come, *we must invent therapy anew for each client.* This is not about finding tools or formulae. It is about responding to the whole person as flexibly as possible.

I most enjoyed a comment from a client—a therapist herself—as we were leaving my work room. She commented upon the smell of cooking coming from the kitchen. I said that I was in the process of making a curry. She smiled, a glint in her eye, and replied: 'And I bet you don't use a recipe either.' I attempt to respond to clients with *considered intuition.*

**Illustrative example**: *Tony was a young man who had been convicted of theft from a local shop. The shop keeper had been his friend. He was distressed by what he had done. Tony had had a difficult relationship with his father, who had subjected him to very harsh* CONDITIONS OF WORTH. *Tony spent a lot of time feeling angry with his father, and then in turn hating himself. He believed that he was a 'no good', as his father kept telling him. I felt that whatever I tried with him in therapy I could not get near to a version of Tony that he could like. I listened to his regret. He really did not want to be found out. I acknowledged his sense of guilt and he agreed. That is what he felt. Then, to my own astonishment, I found myself saying that maybe it was not just about guilt, about doing wrong and being caught at it. Perhaps Tony felt that he had wounded a very precious part of himself. I wanted to reach out to the self-love within Tony that I believed was not yet dead.*

*He looked at me with tear-filled eyes. 'I am so scared that I have damaged something in me that used to be—he hesitated—pure.' The word startled me. By reaching out a little way beyond my own firm understanding of Tony's experience, I had alighted upon a part of him that was scared, but also hopeful. Here we could begin.*

It is from within the conviction that the client is to be met creatively at depth that I want to explore the notion of integration, but it is *person-centred integration* that I want to explore. For a briefer account of this, see Worsley (2004) and for a longer and more detailed exploration of some aspects of this, see Worsley (2002).

## WHAT IS PERSON-CENTRED INTEGRATION? ARE THERE OTHER SORTS?

Firstly, the crucial point to make is that my own, personal approach of person-centred integration is very different from what is normally meant by integrative therapy. It is person-centred. It works on a totally different basis or set of principles to what is normally referred to as integrative therapy.

To begin to grasp the difference I will try, briefly and simply, to paint some of the main characteristics of INTEGRATIVE (and of the closely related ECLECTIC) THERAPIES as I see them. However, if the reader wants to get a fuller view of integration, she might consult Corey (2000), Cully (2004) or O'Brien (2000) as well as the more technical account in Norcross and Arkowitz (1992). I begin with the 'mainstream' meaning of INTEGRATION and ECLECTICISM and then move onto the meaning of person-centred integration.

We cannot escape thinking about integration. We cannot take refuge in some dogmatic version of theory. There are five, personal reasons for me saying this:

1. As a counsellor, I have a number of colleagues who are integrative counsellors (in the mainstream sense). I need to listen to them openly to understand their practice, and to know where I stand in relation to it.
2. The person-centred movement as it is today, is integrative in that it contains a number of 'tribes' while making up one 'nation' (Sanders, 2004). The purist, the integrative practitioner, the experientialist and the FOCUSING practitioner need to understand each other with respect, while knowing why each is distinctive.
3. The person-centred approach is not standing still. New theories are arising from within. These, too, need integrating. (See Chapter 3.)
4. Being CONGRUENT involves my being not just myself, but the

whole of myself. The person who I bring to my clients is the outcome of a process of integration which we more usually refer to as personal development. I hold that there is much in common between this meaning of integration and the more usual one of the integration of theory.

5. I suspect that much of how I am, as integrative, can be seen in CLASSICAL CLIENT-CENTRED counsellors, or at least those who have freed themselves of a certain rigidity. I wish only to make explicit that which for, others, might be implicit.

INTEGRATION is the bringing together of a number of streams of theory into a single, supposedly consistent approach. However, there are several distinct ways of achieving this goal, and the subject is complex (Norcross & Arkowitz, 1992; Sanders, in press). What marks out INTEGRATION in the broader sense is that it tries to help the client by offering a mixture, a recombination of known and familiar schools of therapy. The constituent parts form a new whole. There are things to commend this approach to therapy. Above all, it demonstrates what I hope is obviously the case: *we can learn from other approaches and other individual therapists.* The alternative to this would be unbearably arrogant. However, INTEGRATIVE THERAPIES present us with a number of real problems. These come in two different sorts.

*The first is true INTEGRATION*, as opposed to ECLECTICISM. This involves the making of a new theory out of two or more current theories. There is no reason why the product of this cannot be just as coherent and responsible as any single school of therapy. However, in practice, it is not that simple. Counselling theories are not just random accounts of how to do therapy. They start with a set of principles, a set of beliefs about:

- what it is to be a human being;
- what it is that leaves people distressed and in need of counselling;
- what it is about therapy that is supposed to heal this distress;
- and consequently, what the therapist actually does.

It seems clear to me that if I cannot offer a principled set of answers to these very basic questions, then I literally do not know what I am doing. That leaves my clients at risk, and so is unethical.

Under the banner of INTEGRATION can be found both good practice and very dubious practice indeed. Let us take an example. As I have come to learn a little about integrative counselling courses around in Britain today, I see that INTEGRATION happens in one of two ways. *First*, on some courses, the students are expected to perform their own INTEGRATION and so, in effect, invent their own model. This is very different from becoming idiosyncratically oneself. To become oneself is like developing a driving style that works for you. To have to develop a 'new' therapy while training is like being asked to design and build a car as a way of learning to drive. It is not safe, and would be quite a bizarre way to learn new skills. However, *the second way* is the more responsible. The course team develops, through critical reflection, a model of therapy from which to teach and practice. Yet, even here there is a problem of coherence. For example, if a course combines the person-centred approach with a PSYCHODYNAMIC APPROACH, what are the underlying beliefs of a core model formed from two such opposing methods?

To illustrate: psychodynamic therapists, by and large, believe that useful psychological change happens through therapist interpretation, making available to the client the content of her unconscious. The key concept of healing is that it comes through insight, because the key cause of DYSFUNCTION is REPRESSION of painful material in the unconscious system of the mind. This is part of the PSYCHODYNAMIC APPROACH's basic set of beliefs about being human. To the extent that it is true then therapeutic action based upon it is responsible. By contrast, the person-centred approach is rooted in the belief that the client's ACTUALISING TENDENCY will, given an appropriate environment within therapy, bring about growth to counteract the distorting effects of CONDITIONS OF WORTH upon the SELF-STRUCTURE. These two ways of thinking about therapy are not obviously compatible. The challenge to any INTEGRATIVE THERAPY is to develop a view of humanity and of healing which is coherent, demonstrable and worth believing.

*The second is* ECLECTICISM. This presents another sort of

challenge. ECLECTIC counsellors often think about their skills and knowledge as if they were a tool bag. Any useful technique is then a tool that might be used upon the client. This brings with it a number of major issues:

- The ECLECTIC counsellor chooses what to do at any given point. That is the meaning of ECLECTIC, derived from the Greek for 'I select'. This may threaten the autonomy of the client to take the session where she will, which, as Yalom says above, is at the heart of the relationship.
- What rationale has the counsellor for making a choice? The only possible rationale is clinical 'efficiency', that there is a specific treatment for a specific 'disease'. This moves away from the HOLISM of which Yalom speaks. I doubt the evidence for this as a useful way of thinking. Clients have a wonderful habit of using therapy in surprising ways to produce their own resolutions to their INCONGRUENCE (Bohart & Tallman, 1999).
- The notion of taking hold of a tool, of diagnosis, tends to interrupt the client's whole process. Therapy stops being a DIALOGUE and starts being a clinic.
- To see interventions as tools that can be selected often leads, in practice, to only a superficial understanding of the intervention. I recall speaking to a therapist who said he was ECLECTIC and then added that he was also 'sort-of-person-centred': 'Whenever I don't know what to do, I just reflect what the client has said.' I hope it is obvious to even the least experienced reader of this book that this is a sad and woeful parody of being person-centred (Rogers, 1986).

Person-centred integration is very different from all of this. It is rooted in the principles and beliefs of the person-centred approach. To the extent that it is accurately rooted, it is coherent. What the therapist tries to do is much the same as the CLASSICAL CLIENT-CENTRED THERAPIST, but with a slightly different understanding of the implementation of the SIX CONDITIONS OF THERAPY (Rogers, 1957). What is integrated is any knowledge that helps me understand the client, her process, myself and the therapy. It is integrated into person-centred practice that aims to remain faithful to the core values and insights of the approach. It is remaining person-centred while paying attention to what other insights and approaches contribute to helping me be present to the client with the whole of myself.

In essence, there is no necessary difference between a new insight from within the person-centred approach, such as configurations of self, discussed in Chapter 3; an insight from another model or approach to therapy; and an insight from a novel or a Shakespeare play.

Integration is, in fact, a deliberate *double entendre*: I mean it to have two separate meanings which are both true. Understandings from outside of the model are integrated into practice. However, all that I am and am becoming is integrated, first within myself to the extent that I am whole, and then within my DIALOGUE with the client. It is my intention to bring my whole self into the therapy. Thus, the final chapter of this book is upon the use of the self in counselling. These two meanings sit alongside each other. What I understand and how I understand it becomes part of the person I am. This is true for ideas from other therapeutic approaches. It is true for me for ideas from philosophy and theology. It is true of my experience of watching Shakespeare plays or even soap operas. It is true for my knowledge that comes from being loved and befriended by other people. There is no end to what may become part of me that I may bring to a client. Least of all can I discard the insights of other, competent therapists whom I respect.

In addition to those principles of the person-centred approach set out in Sanders (2004, 2006), I offer four basic principles for person-centred integration:

1. Understand and be clear about your relation to key concepts of person-centred theory. In these, I include in particular the ACTUALISING TENDENCY, the nature of awareness and consciousness, the implications of a commitment to being NON-DIRECTIVE and the meaning of the SIX CONDITIONS of therapy as both necessary and sufficient. These form the basis of the next chapter.
2. Be clear that what are being integrated are concepts and

understandings. How, if at all, these affect practice is for further consideration. We do not integrate techniques wholesale, for therapy is about being and not doing.

3. To understand a concept or idea, you need to have some grasp of its basis in reality. Never be afraid to keep asking what something is *really* about. For example, it is important to grasp that GESTALT therapy shares with person-centred therapy a heritage in PHENOMENOLOGY. Both focus on the lived experience of the client in a way that psychodynamic conceptualisations often do not. Be aware of useful exceptions as well. For instance, group analysis is both psychodynamic and phenomenological (Worsley, 2005).
4. There is no such thing as good, risk-free therapy. Yet, therapy should be safe-enough, for we owe that to our clients. We therefore steer between the devil and the deep, blue sea: between the sense of openness and risk-taking which makes for true DIALOGUE and an obligation to be able to explore and explain what we are doing.

## PERSON-CENTRED INTEGRATION: A PERSONAL HISTORY

When Pete Sanders (2006) started to write *The Person-Centred Counselling Primer*, he was able to talk about the early thoughts of Carl Rogers, its development, its influence by other psychologists and philosophers, and then new thinking after Rogers' death. He describes a school of thought, a whole domain of understanding therapy. By contrast, person-centred integration is quite personal to me. To my knowledge, it has no history, no status beyond my own exploring. This does not mean that others have not trod parallel paths before or after me. Rather, integration, as I describe it, is a personal and idiosyncratic process of pondering and discovery. It is not a model of therapy, but a way of thinking about theory and practice from within the person-centred family. Above all, it is about the freedom to practise as myself while being mindful of my obligation to the client.

What prompted me to thinking about person-centred therapy in an integrative way? Five rather different experiences coincided for me:

1. At the level of theory, I have been influenced by a number of close colleagues whose orientation is certainly not classically client-centred, as well as by colleagues whose approach is classical or purist. Of the latter, I have found that they have been willing to engage and argue with me with respect and energy, and have sharpened my version of remaining person-centred with attention to principle. Of the former, I am unwilling to dismiss their thinking or their practice as either wrong, or so different as to render what they do as foreign to my own spirit of therapy. Therefore I have been forced to ask time and again how the way they think helps me to see the client, myself or therapy in a new or clearer light.
2. I have worked with other therapists in a number of settings—the church, medical general practice, work with the homeless, and now as a university counsellor—as well as supervising other counsellors. I have needed to use the technical language of colleagues of different orientations with respect and understanding (Sommerbeck, 2005). I am aware of the difference I experience between the languages of PSYCHODYNAMIC theory on the one hand and of COGNITIVE-BEHAVIOURAL THERAPY on the other. I feel moderately fluent in the first, whilst in the second I stutter like a novice. To begin to use a language is to enter into a new world of thought. I cannot remain uninfluenced or rejecting of that world. Therefore I concluded that I had to be able to give a responsible account of how others' worlds of thought had affected me, how I had integrated them into my own being. I guess that all of this is true for many CLASSICAL CLIENT-CENTRED therapists, and certainly those who steer clear of a dogmatic rigidity about their work. Maybe all I do is to want to make explicit how understanding therapy and the lived world impacts on relating.
3. I have a real interest in philosophy, having completed a number of years' research in philosophical theology. In addition, poetry and drama were my first loves. I am therefore drawn to ask the question of integration not just about

therapeutic ways of thinking but also about any thinking that attempts to describe what it is to be alive and human. How can I meet a dying person unless I have begun to work through my own dying? This involves diverse activities for me: existential philosophy, poetry and spirituality to name but three.

4. One prompting comes from my time as a counsellor educator. For one term, our diploma course looked at the theory of GESTALT therapy. I was very clear to the students that no amount of 'reading up' would make them, or me, a GESTALT therapist. That would require two to four years of appropriate training. However, GESTALT therapy is beguiling. It is powerful. You can *do* useful things with it. You can direct others in exercises and that's always nice, isn't it? Of course to be beguiled in that way *may be* to give up on the most powerful insights of person-centred practice. Therefore I decided that it was essential to be able to give an account of how this and other therapeutic systems might justifiably affect our thinking while remaining critically engaged with being person-centred. This is part of the freedom to practise.
5. I recognise with pleasure that the different modalities of therapy will, in future, probably grow closer to each other by seeking useful commonalities, common enlightenments. I hope that my personal journey of integration mimics a far more important journey into shared understanding across the approaches.

## WHAT DOES THIS BOOK CONTAIN AND HOW COULD YOU USE IT?

This book is an invitation to think hard about how other theories, other parts of life, affect you as a counsellor, or practitioner of counselling skills. It is important for those who are in training or in practice as counsellors or supervisors. Perhaps it is even more important for those who, for instance, as nurses, teachers and social workers, have to think through the integration of person-centred counselling skills with the core skills of their profession.

Person-centred integration is personal. It is not a system. I have already said that this book, therefore, cannot contain a history of the approach. Each of the main chapters contains comments upon how a particular sort of thinking might affect client work.

The next chapter is of key importance. In it, I examine how to think carefully about some person-centred principles. There then follow four chapters on four pieces of counselling theory which might be integrated into person-centred practice. I want the emphasis to be on practice. Therefore I take only one small aspect of a piece of theory and work with it in detail. I begin with Dave Mearns' rethinking of person-centred theory about the unity of the person. The two chapters which draw on Transactional Analysis and GESTALT therapy remain firmly within the HUMANISTIC THERAPIES and hence PHENOMENOLOGICAL tradition. I move from these to a consideration in Chapter 6 of relationship and meaning from within the EXISTENTIAL tradition.

The seventh chapter is a transcript of a counselling session, and an attempt to set out clearly the relationship of what happens between client and counsellor at the same time as describing what was going on within the counsellor. The book then concludes with explorations of practitioner research as a method for keeping the client safe, and the therapist's use of the self in DIALOGUE.

I intend the main chapters of this book to be examples of good practice, based on careful, even conservative, reflection. I do not want them to be a licence to rush into 'trying something new'. That is to fall back into a mechanistic view of therapy. Real, personal and IDIOSYNCRATIC integration takes time to mature, to sink in. It takes even longer than it takes to learn to cook a half-decent curry!

## WHAT IS OMITTED?

In this book, I make no major reference to my own debt to the PSYCHODYNAMIC tradition. This is mainly a question of space. However a move away from the approaches that share with the PCA its PHENOMENOLOGICAL basis brings with it a new layer of complexity, too. I record with regret that I have had no chance to review here two fascinating areas in particular, in which interdisciplinary dialogue is very much to the fore at this time: object relations theory, as it compares with configurations of self (Chapter 3), and theories of group therapy as this relates, in particular, to group analysis.

## LEVELS OF INTERVENTION

Finally, I want to locate my approach in terms of Margaret Warner's (2000a) levels of intervention. She identifies five levels:

- Level 1: The therapist brings nothing from outside the client's FRAME OF REFERENCE.
- Level 2: The therapist uses personal experiences and theories in order better to understand (but not influence) the client's experience.
- Level 3: The therapist brings material into the relationship in ways that foster the client's choice as to whether, and how, to use such material.
- Level 4: The therapist brings material into the relationship from their own FRAME OF REFERENCE from a position of authority or expertise.
- Level 5: The therapist brings material from outside the client's FRAME OF REFERENCE so that the client is unaware of the intervention, its nature or the therapist's purpose in making the intervention.

(Warner, 2000a: 31, summarized by Sanders, in press)

In brief, I see the therapist who confines herself to Level 1 as probably dogmatic and uncreative. The therapist who is willing to risk Levels 2 and 3 is capable of being integrative. The therapist who uses Levels 4 and 5 is open to a fundamental misunderstanding of the person-centred approach. However, I grant that those who believe that the therapist is the expert on client process are making a responsible Level 4 intervention. No intervention at Level 5 is appropriate, except in those extreme cases where it is necessary to deceive the client, perhaps to preserve her own safety.

I want to end this chapter with some words written to me at

the end of a brief piece of work with someone who had previously fallen into a difficult backwater of our mental health system. I use them with the client's permission. I value them not only because of their personal meaning to me, but also because they express so well what I hope integrative, person-centred therapy feels like:

> *It is difficult to articulate what I've most valued in our meetings, so different from the distant, MEDICAL MODEL I knew. You engaged with me warmly and honestly so I could focus on and spiral round themes painful to me. Being able to be sad in your presence has helped me put down 'things' carried for years. Growth came, in the end, not from reading but from the quirky (to use your term) relationship you offered. It was one of attention, care and collaboration ... trustworthy, one of wisdom.*

We now move on to look at the key, person-centred principles which underlie integration.

# 2

# SOME PERSON-CENTRED PRINCIPLES

> They are the sons and daughters of Life's longing for itself. (Gibran, 1926/1964: 20)

> ... NON-DIRECTIVENESS is an ideally unwavering expression of respect that is manifested *in many and unpredictable ways*, but usually in the form of empathic responses. (Grant, 1990/2002: 376, my italics)

The aim of this chapter is to explore three key pieces of person-centred theory, so as to suggest that this theory is permissive of a wide range of actual actions in counselling. To be person-centred is to be critically flexible and not at all rigid.

The words of the second quotation, above, are from Barry Grant's seminal article on NON-DIRECTIVENESS in person-centred therapy. Yet, the words in italics can be applied to the approach as a whole. There are many and unpredictable ways of implementing a way of being. There are many ways of being empathic. And how can I even begin to think of *a right way* of being CONGRUENT? Acceptance happens within me, first and foremost, and some times I am unaware of how I express it. Yet, in spite of this—which I take to be good news, because it is about the freedom to practise as myself—many beginners are so nervous about their work that they set themselves 'absolutely right' ways of being person-centred. This can sometimes be a means of reassurance. If there is a right way of doing it, then all I need to do is find out what it is and do it. Not so. To find the freedom to practise is to enter into the insecurity of being real and thus taking risks and of not knowing. To make it worse, we should take risks in responsible ways. This is REFLECTIVE PRACTICE. The new counsellor needs to be sure that it is OK to be wrong, for until we can be wrong then we cannot be free. From time to time, courses can instil fear or rigidity when tutors are too afraid or too immersed in pseudo-orthodoxy (Tudor & Worrall, 2004: 1–6). The freedom to practise is the internal freedom of the therapist to respond from their depths to the client. Occasionally I am shocked at what I hear myself say. I do not advocate being shocked or shocking, but with experience, sometimes the unexpected response is truly facilitative of the client because most real.

Do not picture the therapist as impetuous and even self-indulgent. I spend a lot of time in supervision wondering at length how to get useful feelings into the room in an appropriate way. The exciting mystery of therapy for me is that, whether done on the spur of the moment or after long thought with my supervisor, the key question usually comes back to CONGRUENCE: how can I get what I think or feel into the room in a way that is therapeutic. I want to be careful. Yet, I am constantly puzzled by how difficult it is to predict what is a therapeutic way of expressing myself.

I talk above, and in the previous chapter, about taking risks. Sometimes, when I experience myself as at my most real, I am so engaged with the client that I have minimal space available to monitor my responses within the present moment. Yet, my first rule of safety—you will need to think what your basic position on safety for the client is—is that in the beginning of therapy, and especially with a vulnerable client, I am going to put almost all of my energy into a reflective tracking of her, seeking just to understand how it is for her. At the same time I will put conscious energy into thinking about how safe she feels within her own process and with me. It is when we get to know each other and there is some groundedness within the client—her confidence in her, and our, process—that I move towards what I think of as a more vigorous dialogue. The basic point is made for me by Maria Villas-Boas Bowen:

> Forty-five years later we hear [Carl Rogers] verbalizing attitudes that the client has not yet introduced, offering and testing interpretations, and often being quite directive with the client. I think the biggest change of all is that he trusted the client more. He considered them to be less fragile and less easily damaged by comments made by the therapist. (Villas-Boas Bowen, 1996: 94)

Since there are no rules that tell me what to *do* in therapy, but only principles that tell me how to *be*, then I need to have a critical grasp of these principles, so that I may steer between the rigid and the sloppy with responsibility, creativity and freedom. What follows is a consideration of three themes that will prove crucial in the process of integration.

## THE ACTUALISING TENDENCY

Why we do things (motivation) is an important area of interest in psychology. In 1963, Carl Rogers was one of a number of speakers to address the 11th Nebraska Symposium on Motivation. The previous year, one of the speakers was the famous behaviourist, Albert Bandura. Rogers was well aware that BEHAVIOURISM seems to give a detailed, diagnostic account of the interaction of behaviour and the surrounding world. It divides up motivation into a number of constituent elements. Rather like ECLECTICISM, it tries to tie particular causes of lack of motivation to particular treatments or tactics. For classical BEHAVIOURISM, motivation is inhibited by this or that force. For example, an anorexic young girl who eats so little that her body weight falls until it gets close to threatening her life as well as her health might be seen as being driven by a mis-learning about her body image. This specific change in her COGNITIVE-BEHAVIOURAL pattern creates an increased tension, or inhibition, in the individual. To reshape behaviour is to reduce this tension.

Rogers' (1963) paper offers precisely the opposite view. For Rogers, to be in healthy process is to be in touch with a *constructive* tension within the organism. He begins the paper with a memory of walking along the California coast. There he saw, near the shoreline, what at first seemed to be a large number of miniature palm trees. He had never seen the like before. Overcome with curiosity, he went down to look at these strange plants. They turned out to be a species of seaweed which specialises in growing at the water margin, that hostile environment where waves eternally beat against rocks. This variety of seaweed had evolved a structure in which the fronds had become woven together to form sturdy trunks to hold the more tender parts of the plant clear of the force of the waves. Rogers recognised that nature had created a particular form of plant that would inhabit one of the least hospitable of environments.

Rogers' whole theory of personality is based on the notion that what motivates us is not a decrease in tension, but an increase, a formative, or creative, force (Rogers, 1959). Life evolves in the universe, in spite of its entropy (the tendency to run down to a dead flatness on a cosmic scale) because there is a powerful tendency for complexity to increase on smaller scales. Thus, inorganic activity moves towards being organic; plant life moves towards animal life. This is the directional or formative tendency. In human beings and in other forms of life, this takes on a particular type of constructive activity. The ACTUALISING TENDENCY is, at its most general, the ability of any organism to achieve its potential for growth. Thus, with the seaweed that Rogers encountered, it had, over evolutionary time, expressed its potential in the forming of a structure of 'self' that allowed it to survive the hostility of wave power.

Person-centred therapy is rooted in this fact. Human beings, given an adequate environment, will realise their own potential for growth. Thus the practitioner must never get in the way of this fundamental process so as to arrest it. Whatever is integrated into our thinking about therapy, the consequent behaviour of the therapist over time must leave the client the space and freedom to grow.

For some (but not all) CLASSICAL CLIENT-CENTRED THERAPISTS a minimalist offering of the CORE CONDITIONS is the way to ensure this freedom to grow. It is certainly the case that an accurate and loving tracking of the client is valuable in this process. However, it is an error to presume that only the classical form of person-centred practice is 'true' in relation to the client's ACTUALISING TENDENCY. Therapy is ENCOUNTER (Schmid, 1998); it is two people meeting. Within this, there is room for varied and unexpected behaviours. As Maria Villas-Boas Bowen notes, above, Carl Rogers also came to see the client as more robust than he had in earlier days. There will be marked differences in robustness between clients, and FRAGILE PROCESS has to be worked with carefully and tenderly. Yet other clients can be encountered with vigour. It is an error to tie reliance on the ACTUALISING TENDENCY to one form of person-centred practice. However, the integrative practitioner must take particular care to remain on a shared journey with the client, allow the client to discover her path forward and prepare to be surprised.

> **Illustrative example**: *When Geoffrey came to me, he was not only angry and depressed with life at home, but he had found his doctor, a previous counsellor and his referral to a psychiatrist very difficult. Each had offered him a different label for his unhappiness. He commented wryly that he had little confidence in them if they could not even agree on a label. His question was a serious one. Can my experience be taken seriously? This tapped into strong views within me. I checked that I was not about to embark on a self-indulgent pursuit of a hobby horse of my own. I came to the conclusion that Geoffrey was 'inviting' me to say whether I could take his experience seriously or not. We had quite a long debate—45 minutes over two sessions—about the nature of depression. While I do not often begin therapy with a piece of psychological education, it seemed to me that Geoffrey was seeking from within himself to be met on his own, and not his doctor's, terms. I reflect that an unusual piece of behaviour on my part felt to be a valid response to Geoffrey's actualising tendency.*

## PRINCIPLED NON-DIRECTIVENESS

In the 1940s, Carl Rogers had referred to what he did as NON-DIRECTIVE THERAPY. Subsequently, he and others have come to see that being NON-DIRECTIVE is only one element of a facilitative relationship. Sometimes, I am more directive in a specific moment than the CCC therapist would be. Each instant must be judged for itself. There is no simple criterion that will keep clients and their counsellors 'safe'. If I am directive, it will be as part of a potentially risky, but holistic, response to the client as a complete person. It is an error to see the whole matter of directiveness as being resolvable by appeal to the alleged difference between content and process, with the therapist as an expert on process but not content. This stance is often taken by EXPERIENTIAL therapists, such as Rennie (1998). Very often clients have real expertise on their own process, and at other times they have not. The same is true of their content.

In 1990, Barry Grant published an influential paper (Grant, 1990/2002) in which he distinguished between two ways of being NON-DIRECTIVE: the principled way and the instrumental way. Instrumental NON-DIRECTIVENESS involves seeing each intervention, each therapist comment, as an example of 'being non-directive' and therefore useful. This sort of NON-DIRECTIVENESS is a deliberate, if very subtle, influencing of the client. NON-DIRECTIVENESS in this case is seen as a tool, something that the therapist *does* to the client. It is not genuine, because it is at odds with a person-centred intention to encounter the client as whole human being.

By contrast, principled NON-DIRECTIVENESS is rooted in the conviction that the whole relationship is to be NON-DIRECTIVE, and that this is an ethical commitment. It is about the therapist's overall attitude. I want to encounter the client as she is. I do not want to think about using a curative technique called *being NON-DIRECTIVE*. It is an ethical stance: to be directive is wrong because it robs the client of her moment-by-moment autonomy and because it tends to set the therapist in a radically expert role. This is Grant's argument and I find it valuable.

Yet, to be NON-DIRECTIVE in a principled way is to see the therapeutic relationship not only as ethical but also as whole and not an infinite series of brief moments. NON-DIRECTIVENESS is, then, not something that I can switch on or off. It is a subtle quality of a whole relationship. But it is not absolute. I can never be wholly NON-DIRECTIVE. I fall short even by a look, a glance, a facial expression. I have argued elsewhere (Worsley, 2002: 40–6) that there can be no such thing as absolute NON-DIRECTIVENESS. Whatever I say, notice, respond to, remain silent about in the other, I necessarily preclude other things that I might have said or done. This influences the client. Sometimes, I do this quite deliberately, to challenge the client: Did you hear what you just said? Sometimes my hearing of one word in preference to another can have major consequences in the flow of conversation. I believe that we delude ourselves if we think of NON-DIRECTIVENESS in this way. While the principle of HORIZONTALISATION requires us to attempt to listen equally to all that the client says (Spinelli, 1989: 18–23; Worsley, 2002: 61), the therapeutic conversation is always influenced by what we hear or do not hear. Sometimes selective hearing or selective responding cannot be avoided. At other times therapists fall victim to moments of bias, deafness, prejudice and therapeutic bright ideas.

Being NON-DIRECTIVE is about the quality of a whole relationship, about trust, about the therapist conveying non-directive *intent*, and about the ability of the client to maintain her LOCUS OF EVALUATION. All of these are variables, and interlink in a complex fashion.

Thus, it is possible to negotiate or otherwise undertake some sorts of seemingly directive actions within a relationship that remains fundamentally NON-DIRECTIVE. The therapist has a degree of freedom to take risks while remaining true to the principle of NON-DIRECTIVENESS. In acting in any particular way, the therapist needs to bear in mind the following questions:

1. Where in the relationship are we? Should I still be offering maximal safety? How do I know that a challenge is safe enough?
2. How do I know that the client can meet me at a particular level of vigour? How is her LOCUS OF EVALUATION, generally? With me?
3. What is it within me that wants to take a particular course with the client?

The last of these is of particular importance. In the illustrative example below, I had in mind some concepts from GESTALT therapy, but also some concepts from the work of Eugene Gendlin. Both speak about feelings being *EMBODIED*, or manifest as real physical sensations. How we EMBODY feeling is important, (See Chapter 5) so what mattered for me was whether I was in some sense 'hooked' on these ideas or whether I was free to use them appropriately so as to forward my empathic grasp of the client's world, including his EMBODIED world.

**Illustrative example**: *It had taken Robert a long while to talk of his fear. Fear for him was unmanly. He felt ashamed. I wanted to reflect three aspects of his experience to him. He was afraid. I could feel that with him. He was ashamed of this. As I acknowledged that, I thought I felt the level of shame both increase—he blushed markedly—but also become more acceptable, or at least open, to him. He no longer had to conceal it. After a while, I became intrigued about his embodiment of fear. Did he fully feel it or was it blocked? I asked him directly how he felt it. For some clients the notion of felt-sense is not part of their normal repertoire, but for Robert it seemed to be. He described fear as a hot torrent running from his head to his solar plexus. I had been directive. I had pointed with empathic curiosity to the possibly missing third element in his experience. If Robert had backed away from this, I would have done so too. He did not. Between us we had a new element of language, felt and forming within him and between us. Directiveness in the moment was safely contained within a NON-DIRECTIVE relationship.*

## THE NECESSARY AND SUFFICIENT CONDITIONS OF THERAPY

In 1957, Carl Rogers published a paper in the *Journal of Consulting Psychology* which set out with clarity his answer to the question: Why does person-centred therapy work? A summary of this paper can be found in Sanders (2006: 7–10). I do not intend to repeat this material here, but to point to one particular issue arising from the use of this paper. I take Rogers' work always to be exploratory, an attempt to frame his practice and theory with precision, but provisionally. In later life he would express regret that he might have underestimated the importance of some elements, or that others had used his work as if it were written in tablets of stone.

My sole concern here is to debug integration of the accusation that what is integrated is a series of techniques which implicitly deny the necessity and sufficiency of the SIX THERAPEUTIC CONDITIONS. A technique is a tool, a thing we do, a set of instructions, a PROTOCOL. ECLECTICISM thinks in this way: My client has Goldfish syndrome, and my therapy manual says that visualising a tank of water being drained might be helpful. So let's get on with it and see what happens. By contrast, person-centred therapy is about relating, and that in turn rests on a set of therapist attitudes and values. Rogers' SIX CONDITIONS are an attempt to sum up what these attitudes and values might be in practice. They deserve respect as authoritative contributions to a debate, but they are not to be seen as absolute authorities.

In particular, I want to look at two aspects of the SIX CONDITIONS: their logical status and their practical status. Only in this way will we come to understand their practical *purpose* in counselling.

A set of conditions in therapy is said to be necessary when it is the case that the outcome—in this case, constructive personality change (Rogers, 1957: 95)—can only happen if these conditions are present. The conditions are said to be sufficient when it is the case that the outcome always happens whenever the conditions are in place. Many therapists respond to Rogers' idea by taking the view that the conditions *are* necessary but *not* sufficient, and so we must do something else, something more, something better. Person-centred therapists rightly resist this, because it is a profound misunderstanding of the approach. Whatever we do, we do not *add in* mere techniques. To this I happily subscribe. Yet, I sometimes find myself accused of not adhering to the SIX CONDITIONS because I think I might learn something from the GESTALT therapist, Fritz Perls, or whoever.

Rogers was a first-rate scientist. He knew what 'necessary and sufficient' means. He would not make claims that are patently ridiculous. Yet, if we take 'necessary and sufficient' literally, we make a very difficult claim. That the SIX CONDITIONS are necessary is seen as being non-controversial by many. Why? Jerold Bozarth (1998, Chapter 5) has argued that they are not necessary at all. Many other conditions in life promote constructive personality change. It is evidence of the ACTUALISING TENDENCY that this is so. For example, Viktor Frankl (2004) has described in great detail how, in his experience of being in a Nazi concentration camp, it is the ability to find meaning that leads to survival rather than death.

Meaning is key, more so than food, warmth or whatever. The SIX CONDITIONS are not, strictly speaking, logically necessary for psychological growth. It is even more obvious that to say they are sufficient is a hostage to fortune. We would only need *one example* of constructive growth happening without the six conditions to demonstrate that they are NOT logically sufficient. So where now?

Rogers' argument is a practical one, an act of exploration. He is saying that what heals is embedded in relating, in encounter, which in turn relies upon a quality of meeting and that in turn relies upon a set of therapist attitudes. So, then we can ask what defines techniques. A technique is that which is contrary to, not rooted in, basic qualities and attitudes in the therapist. A technique is trickery. Its opposite is genuineness.

Whatever I learn, or do, as a result of my encounter with other approaches to counselling, it must be rooted in encounter. It ought to be describable with honesty under the terms of the SIX CONDITIONS. It must be genuine. Rogers (1986) complains bitterly that 'reflection of feelings' which might seem so empathic is in fact not genuine because it is a technique rather than an integrated way of being. When I think carefully about the SIX CONDITIONS OF THERAPY, I recognise the freedom to integrate, to make whole my practice, as a way of being intuitive, IDIOSYNCRATIC and alive.

## In conclusion

So far in this chapter I have examined three main strands of theory which are the foundations of person-centred practice. By continually asserting that this practice is about relationship and therapist-attitude, I have countered a number of objections to person-centred integration that it is not true to theory. At the same time, I have opened up ways of thinking about what can be integrated from other theoretical bases that are also expressions of a person-centred way of being.

In a number of the following chapters, controversial ideas from other schools of therapy will be encountered. Sometimes the person-centred community exhibits a sort of shared insecurity by being suspicious about theory that is not patently from within itself. This is an unhelpful attitude. It develops into a state whereby some take it upon themselves to police others.

I remember going to a half-day conference at which the speaker was the doyen of person-centred couple therapists, Charles O'Leary. He is an engaging speaker who in presenting material dramatises what he is doing brilliantly. One member of the audience questioned him carefully about how he offered empathy to both members of a warring couple. It seemed a fascinating exploration. Suddenly the young questioner turned on O'Leary with a sort of triumph: 'So, you don't believe in the sufficiency of the SIX CONDITIONS, then?' O'Leary stopped, hand to mouth, in fake astonishment. He became a clown: 'Well, you've really got old Charlie there, haven't you? What can I say? I think I can say [pause] that I don't find your question at all helpful.'

O'Leary's point is that the young questioner was not looking with intelligent openness to what O'Leary actually does or intends. They were making a point, policing him.

The point of thinking theoretically is to grow, not to demonstrate to those who want to police us that we are adequately orthodox. I suggest that in integrating other theoretical insights into person-centred counselling, the litmus test is whether the resulting therapy is in accord with the theory of the ACTUALISING TENDENCY of the client; the principled non-directivity of the whole relationship; and the SIX CONDITIONS of therapy as an expression of a HOLISTIC, IDIOSYNCRATIC and responsive encounter with another human being. It is possible and useful to integrate others' insights, not as laws written in tablets of stone, but as concepts, sometimes quite slippery, but fascinating to play with. How they touch upon the practice of therapy is a matter of some subtle judgement.

Such encounters happen in unusual ways and unusual places. In the example below, I suggest that a moment in teaching a violinist how to think about what she was doing makes my point precisely. Consider what Joy Farrell does in terms of the three principles considered in this chapter.

**Illustrative example**: *I recently attended, as an observer, a master class given by Joy Farrell. She is Professor of Clarinet at the Guildhall School of Music in London. I watched her with fascination. She is a lovely teacher. With the clarinettist, she had a gentle authority, suggestive, supportive, warm, firm and tender. In short, I saw the* CORE CONDITIONS *in action. The five young Cambridge musicians were working on the Mozart Clarinet Quintet in A major (K581). At one point, she stopped the performance and turned to the first violinist. She explained that woodwind performers often do not understand string techniques. She asked why the violinist had bowed a passage in a particular way. The violinist explained. It seemed as if this was simply accepted. The music continued. After a couple of minutes, she stopped them again and asked why it had now been done differently, and better. She had only asked a question about it and no more. What had happened? The lead violinist looked puzzled but knew what Joy was referring to. The difference was clear if puzzling. The learning was never made explicit but was facilitated by the teacher, and found by the learner from within her own resources, her own expertise.*

# 3

# INTEGRATING NEW THINKING IN PERSON-CENTRED THEORY: CONFIGURATIONS OF SELF

I want to look at Dave Mearns and Brian Thorne's concept of configurations of self. Dave and Brian are by now much-respected, elder statesmen of the British, person-centred community; yet, we must nevertheless presume that their new insight is in need of some justification. Does it fit? What does integrating it mean?

Whenever new insights arise, the old familiar pattern of theory changes. This is disturbing. Is the new useful? Does it challenge or concord with the central principles?

## THE SELF AS SINGLE

The West, throughout nearly a thousand years, has had a disconcerting habit of seeing its world-view as unique and superior to that of others. Yet, parts of its world-view have been riddled with error. It seems to me intuitively obvious that I am I, a person, the Single One. PLATONIC THOUGHT has tended to see humans as single points of abstract existence, sometimes referred to as souls. This way of thinking was confirmed by the work of the French scientist and philosopher, René Descartes (1596–1650). For him, mind and soul became a single point of CONSCIOUSNESS, abstract in that it was not extended in space. Nobody was concerned to know how the mind and the brain actually interacted. While few (though there are notable exceptions) would hold anything like Descartes' view of mind today, the habit of thinking of ourselves as single persists.

It is not surprising that Carl Rogers went with this quirk of Western thought, the self as unitary, a single system. However there is more to it than just history, for Rogers' version of the self as single has subtlety. The fifteenth of Rogers' NINETEEN PROPOSITIONS reads as follows:

> Psychological adjustment exists when the concept of the self is

> such that all the sensory and visceral experience of the organism are, or may be, assimilated on a symbolic level into a consistent relationship with the concept of the self. (Rogers, 1951: 513)

Rogers' view of the self is not unitary in the way that Descartes' is.

Rogers' major division is between the ORGANISMIC VALUING PROCESS and the SELF-CONCEPT. The ORGANISMIC VALUING PROCESS is inherent in all human beings. It is the process of taking in and assessing experiences of the world around us. When uninhibited, this process can be felt at gut level as a sensing that one or another experience should be evaluated. If we could live by this alone, there would be well-being. However, as we experience CONDITIONS OF WORTH, imposed from outside of ourselves, we develop a SELF-CONCEPT, an idea of how we are. This is a mental representation to ourselves of how we *believe* we are. It includes those conditions that we take in—INTROJECT—and so is that aspect of self which adapts unnaturally to surrounding demands. It is in this division between the ORGANISMIC VALUING PROCESS and the SELF-CONCEPT that INCONGRUENCE is manifest. However, it is crucial for Rogers' thinking how there is but one motivational force for health: the ACTUALISING TENDENCY. Thus, he tends to see the personality as a whole, an organism which can grow and overcome the 'fracture' of INCONGRUENCE.

It is essential to Rogers' thinking that the personality is seen as a single entity, as a reaction to Freud, who saw the personality as divided into three structural entities: the Superego, the Ego and the Id. It is only after this holistic view is well embedded in person-centred thinking that the approach can notice that the whole also manifests subdivisions beyond those postulated by Rogers. Mearns' work on configurations of self is necessarily subsequent to Rogers' thinking.

If this brief overview is at all accurate, then we see another purpose to integration. The theory of therapy proceeds not by proclaiming a ready-formed truth, but by a dialectical process (a process in which each element modifies its predecessor and is modified by that which follows). This sets out one emphasis that is both true and useful, but not absolutely so, and then encounters a second, modifying emphasis which, if also useful and true, shifts and refines the overview of theory. This process of refinement, of DIALOGUE, of conversation, is one of judgement or estimation and has a gradual and organic feel to it. It means that integration is necessary to the organic life of thought. It is my belief that Mearns and Thorne's work on configurations of self exemplifies this healthy and organic process of a community learning.

## Configurations of self

In 1994, Professor Dave Mearns of the University of Strathclyde published a brief case study of a client, Elizabeth (Mearns, 1994: 12–16). He describes how he came to understand Elizabeth in a way that could not readily be fully expressed in terms of person-centred theory as it then stood.

Mearns' case study aims to encourage us to offer the CORE CONDITIONS to all parts of the client. This is very much in tune with the work done in the previous decade by John Rowan (1990) in exploring what he had termed 'subpersonalities'. Rowan knew that people had a folk awareness of the rather exotic condition often referred to as 'dissociative identity disorder', in which the personality fragments into a number of 'selves' which seem to be quite cut off from each other. However, he was struck by the fact that a possibly different, but certainly far more normal, condition existed in which people could identify a number of subsystems within their 'self' and name them, and work with them. After practical research in workshops, Rowan claimed that many people could typically identify six subpersonalities, with as many as fifty being reported by some.

While Mearns and Rowan offer similar descriptions of the same phenomenon—as I take it to be—it is Mearns' writing about Elizabeth that brought it to widespread recognition in person-centred theory.

Elizabeth had experienced a number of CONDITIONS OF WORTH, which she had survived with into her forties, before seeking help.

Mearns describes them thus:

- You are good if you are caring
- You are not good if you express dissent
- Crying for yourself is selfish
- You are evil if you hurt your mother
- You are evil if you hurt your father
- Your value is in the service you give others
- Second best is failure

(Mearns, 1994: 13)

What Mearns notes is that the INCONGRUENCE between the SELF-CONCEPT and the ORGANISMIC VALUING PROCESS is more complex than a single conflict. Elizabeth is able to identify three configurations within herself. The 'nun' is the version of her self who obeys the CONDITIONS OF WORTH: I am caring and so I love my clients, etc. However there also exists a 'little girl' who embodies the need to stand out against this tyrannous regime. The 'little girl' does so by expressing the exact opposite of the 'nun': I don't really care and so I despise my clients, myself, my husband and so I am a sham. Notice here how the ACTUALISING TENDENCY as I understand it works in a remarkable way. It would have been possible for Elizabeth to have just become the little girl, and really despised her clients, for example. Yet, there is the plunge into depression. The little girl is not just in rebellion but senses that the counter-identity she puts out will not do. She *is* a sham! In other words, depression as a signal of INCONGRUENCE is highly functional. It prevents Elizabeth from becoming a real sham by dragging her down, for the time being, into self-despair. This is based upon a valid estimate of 'the nun' as being a sham, but remains highly unrealistic about the whole of her self being a sham.

The process of depression faced in therapy—as it can be in everyday life—brings into being a third aspect of Elizabeth, in which feeling bad is a beginning to the recognition of the reality of the situation. Mearns characterises Elizabeth's process of self-reconciliation in these terms:

- I am really struggling with all of this
- I am crying for *me* nowadays

> • This depression feels totally different from before. It feels much blacker and I feel fully *in* it rather than fighting it
> (Mearns, 1994: 14)

It is in entering into the blackness of depression that begins a process of reconciliation. It could be described in terms of a reduction of INCONGRUENCE as the defendedness of Elizabeth gives way to recognition of conflicting urges. Another way to think of it would be in terms of the relationship between the 'nun' and the 'little girl' as having the potential for reconciliation.

Six years after Mearns published this case study, he put out, together with Brian Thorne, a fuller account of configurations of self (Mearns & Thorne, 2000: 101–43). This is important reading, not least in its description of how the concept affects their therapeutic practice. However, I want to bear in mind for the discussion below, the definition that they offer of a configuration:

> A 'configuration' is a hypothetical construct denoting a coherent pattern of feelings, thoughts and preferred behavioural responses symbolised or pre-symbolised by the person as reflexive of a dimension of existence within the Self. (Mearns & Thorne, 2000: 102)

## DISCUSSION

The definition of a configuration which Mearns and Thorne offer is by no means easy. Let us think what it points to. Mearns prefers the idea of a configuration rather than a 'part' of a client (Mearns & Thorne, 2000: 102), because the word configuration suggests that each configuration contains an internal dynamic. That is, each configuration can exhibit the tension between the ORGANISMIC VALUING PROCESS and the SELF-CONCEPT. Yet, a configuration is a hypothetical construct. That is, any particular configuration, like 'the nun', is an idea which might come from the client or the therapist or both, which is a naming of a complex set of actual phenomena gathered from the client's experience of their life. There is no claim that there is a discrete part of the mental structure marked for ever as 'the nun'. The construct represents, to the pair in DIALOGUE, the client's way of classifying her experience. For the client, 'the nun' exists at that time. But, it exists not just as a fantasy. It points to a set of feelings, thoughts and behaviours which are coherent: they belong together. We might hypothesise that there is, within the meaning-structure of the brain, a very complex set of linkages which allow these feelings and actions to communicate fluently, or, in Rowan's (1990) terms, to act as a subpersonality.[1] There are sets of feelings, thoughts and actions which belong together within the client.

Any configuration can be symbolised or pre-symbolised. The word SYMBOLISATION is used by Carl Rogers (1951: 513, for example) to stand for the process of an experience moving into consciousness. There are configurations, or patterns of affect (feelings) and action, of which in varying degrees the client is not conscious.[2] When a particular configuration becomes more consciously available to the client, then two things happen. The client develops a higher level of REFLEXIVITY (Rennie, 2006) and, hence, of access to meaning. When Elizabeth can think of a configuration of feelings and behaviours as 'the nun' she can address it at the level of its meaning. However, meaning and interpretation are not the whole point. The material moves into conscious awareness and is thus processed more slowly. This allows it to emerge into awareness slowly and persistently.

Clients are often puzzled, disorientated or even frightened when they experience themselves as multiple. To be able to work with configurations of self is reassuring. What they experience is, as Rowan (1990) argued, quite normal. At the same time the content and the process of their configurations become more

---

1. While it is way beyond the range of this book to go, in detail, into the neuroscience, Gerald Edelman (1992) puts forward a mechanism that he terms high-level re-entrant mapping, which might go a long way to explain how some meaning-structures communicate fluently while others are isolated from each other.

2. I prefer the word conscious here, not in order to be Freudian but to refer to Gray's (2004) discussion of the processing speeds of conscious and unconscious material.

available to them—they are symbolised—so that they can be worked with. The third element in Mearns' case study, the element of reconciliation, outlines one of a very large number of precise processes by which INCONGRUENCE is reduced.

There are a number of practical consequences of working with configurations of self. We need to remain aware that a configuration is a construct, an idea, an interpretation of a set of phenomena. It is not a 'thing'. We may not presume that it will persist over time. It is nearer to a METAPHOR and so deserves to be treated with caution. It also deserves respect.

Mearns' first intention in 1994 was to help us offer the CORE CONDITIONS to each and every part of the client.

**Illustrative example**: Megan had been having panic attacks as the examinations approached. The more she panicked the worse she felt in case she failed the second year of her degree. The tension within her was palpable. Every muscle seemed to strain after success. The fear was clear as well. She pleaded with me to help her get through these exams. Every bit of her strove for this goal. Or did it? Sometimes we seek actively to undermine our own efforts. Yet to offer an interpretation like that can seem quite punitive. I guessed that not all of Megan wanted to succeed. I knew that her father, a cold and withholding man, could inspire a level of real fear in her. He was genuinely scary! I took the risk of trying to empathise with another part of her self. 'I guess, with a Dad like yours, it is pretty annoying having to pass absolutely everything, if you want any warmth from him at all.' Her eyes filled with tears. There was, though, a calmness about her. 'I just hate jumping through his hoops!' There was within her a battle. I too wanted to see her spite him. I could feel the battle inside me too.

In this example, there is a real risk. Sometimes clients will refer fully to the configuration by themselves. To work with it is to remain within the known FRAME OF REFERENCE of the client. At other times, the therapist may have a very good idea of 'something else' with which to empathise. It is important to be hesitant and tender, never to explore with psychological heavy-handedness.

How does the concept of configurations of self fit with person-centred theory? Its main challenge is to the notion of the unity of the self, and in particular the unity of the SELF-CONCEPT. Paradoxically, the SELF-CONCEPT, in that it is plural like 'the nun' and 'the little girl', is not just a consciously held idea of who we are. The SELF-CONCEPT needs to be seen as both within and beyond conscious awareness. It needs to be seen as more DIALOGICAL and more organic than the rather concretely cognitive notion of a concept, a rational idea. Above all, once we have let go of the unity of self, the payoff is to get a greater understanding of the very complexity of our ways of minimising our INCONGRUENCE. The plurality of self and depression resulting from INCONGRUENCE is, in a way, a functional pattern, a method we learn in order to cope with our greater discomfort. Elizabeth had indeed survived until she was forty-something. The complex pattern that plurality weaves has true survival potential. Mental distress comes to look less like a disease and more like a pattern of human awareness with both pluses and minuses (Sanders, 2005).

**Illustrative example**: *The following is taken from an article by Matthew Campling (2006: 31) in which he describes, not therapy, but how he used two of his configurations to move away from anorexia nervosa himself:*

The best way to describe what happened was that I split myself into two selves: the anorexic self and the healthy self. The healthy self knew I was in great danger, that if I didn't find a way to get healthy, I would become seriously ill. I had an insight into the anorexic self, the tyrant, which I have not read in any papers on the subject: the anorexic self was terrified.

The tyrant wasn't so much a bully as in mortal fear. Because if I got well, then the anorexic self would die. It being impossible to contemplate our own demise, the anorexic self was prepared to starve me to death rather than give up control. Also, the anorexic self did not know how to help, only to control and deny.

But the healthy self had an idea. Exercise had become very important to me over the last few years. The healthy self made a pact with the anorexic: in order to exercise, which the anorexic self liked, I would need to eat. Rather than the method which I had heard expressed by eating experts that 'normal eating patterns must be resumed' the anorexic self allowed the healthy self a certain amount of control. But all the while, the healthy self was pursuing its own agenda: to put a few more pounds on my frame.

*My thanks go to Matthew for his permission to use this excerpt.*

Like all good theory, configurations of self theory links with other concepts and suggests further thinking and development. Mearns and Thorne (2000: 136–8) suggests that there is a family of selves, and that, while this is only a METAPHOR, it is still a useful mirror of the actual family of the client. This is true. However, group analysis had got there somewhat in advance (Chazan, 2001, Chapter 5 and especially p. 56). The plurality of self suggests even more the group. Group therapy may resonate very well with thinking about configurations. How do my configurations link with others in the group? There is more and richer diversity than at first appears. There is also useful thinking to be done about Mearns and Thorne's observation that the plurality–family link is *only* a METAPHOR. Our selves come into being through our being in groups and families, firstly by relating with our prime carers and then through wider socialisation. It seems to me, at first sight, that there will be an organic link between internal and external plurality—the selves and the group or family.

The integration of the new into person-centred theory, even from 'within', leads to exciting prospects for understanding the self and its links to society, groups, families and development during early life.

## IN CONCLUSION

The theory of configurations of self is wholly compatible with the foundational belief in the ACTUALISING TENDENCY, and may describe in some detail how the client has striven to self-actualise. The relationship between the different configurations can be seen as, in varying degrees, functional or DYSFUNCTIONAL. It is Dave Mearns' (1994) key point that the construct helps the therapist offer the CORE CONDITIONS more fully, more subtly, to the whole of the client and not just to that which is verbally obvious. Indeed, the new theory is pregnant with possibilities for future thinking about clients and their families and other social groups. It is one sign of a good theory in all disciplines that it is capable of generating more developed thinking, further new theory. However, the theory of configurations presents a significant challenge in practice. Because different configurations subsist at different levels of awareness within the client at different times, there is careful judgement to be made about how directive (if at all) the counsellor is prepared to be in pointing to, or empathising with, configurations which are not immediately within the client's awareness at a particular point in time. As I have argued in Chapter 2, there is no simple, right answer here. I feel freer to take risks when the client feels safe and is grounded and able to respond to me openly and CONGRUENTLY.

# 4

# THE SPACE BETWEEN PEOPLE: EGO-STATE THEORY

This chapter looks to Transactional Analysis (TA) and in particular its construct of Parent–Adult–Child. I will ask what this can teach us about human relating. I am, as ever, not interested in tools, of tricks of the trade. I want nothing to do with therapy by PROTOCOL. This will be a test of careful integration, to avoid the instrumental nature of some TA practice while using the insight from TA theory.

TA has sold itself with merciless commercial acumen. It has been a powerful force in corporate training in industry on both sides of the Atlantic. Eric Berne's (1964/1968) little book, *Games People Play*, has taken psychology into the realms of the middle-class supper party. Read it and you need never be bored with your friends again! Meanwhile, Harris' (1970/1973) bestseller, *I'm OK–You're OK*, is made to seem racy and commercial. It advertises itself with the slogan: 'Climb out of the cellar of you mind … '. While I have taught TA theory for many years, my idea of what a TA therapist *does* is still rather hazy. I much enjoyed Pete Sanders' deeply ironic comment to me that there is a good fit between the person-centred approach and TA, because a therapy without a theory meets a theory without a therapy. (I hope that even the least experienced reader will note that the stereotype of person-centred therapy as being 'light on theory' is a crass misunderstanding! Hence the irony.) By now, I hope you are asking yourself: Why should I take TA at all seriously?

The answer for me is that, in spite of the popularising tone of some of its books (but see Clarkson, 1992, for a truly scholarly account), Eric Berne, its founding father, has made a serious and useful contribution to counselling psychology. He has offered a PHENOMENOLOGICAL account of patterns of human relationships which have the capacity to illuminate how behaviour in the individual, CONDITIONS OF WORTH and behaviour in groups can be relatively easily conceptualised.

## Psychological theory as a language to use

In this chapter, I will concentrate upon one of Berne's constructs, Parent–Adult–Child (PAC).[1] I will set out the simpler, functional model (Stewart & Joines, 1987, Chapter 3). I will then ask how it sits with PHENOMENOLOGY, and lastly put forward two ways in which it can be integrated into PERSON-CENTRED THERAPY.

The first mode of integration is simple enough. The EGO-STATE model attributes to people three states of mind: Parent, Adult and Child. Sometimes we are said to be 'in Child' (TA enjoys jargon!). In this state, some of our thinking, feeling and behaving will be deeply influenced by how we were as children, and by the role of the child in society. This state of mind is reflected in body language. Therefore a sympathetic grasp of EGO-STATES theory can alert the therapist to certain quirks and signs in the client of their functioning. To the extent that EGO-STATE theory works, this is not controversial. It is merely a learning to look.

The second mode of integration is more controversial. It is a way in which the therapist and the client can use PAC to think about TRANSACTIONS between themselves or between the client and a third party. PAC then has the quality of being a language. It can become a way of expressing and thinking about and looking at behaviours in relationship. Language communicates. Language also empowers. If this language can be of help to the client, should it be seen as different from any other language?

## Parent–Adult–Child

Eric Berne described an EGO STATE as 'a consistent pattern of feeling and experience, directly related to a corresponding consistent pattern of behaviour' (Berne, 1966, Chapter 10). This definition bears a number of similarities to definitions of configurations of self (see above, Chapter 3). However, there is a major difference to note. Mearns' notion of a configuration is that it is unique to

1. I will use the convention of capitalising the ego states and retaining lower case initials for the normal meaning of these three words.

each individual. Only the individual can finally be sure that a particular configuration (as concept) truly applies to her. Berne, though, works at a level of greater generalisation. We have to decide, within ourselves as practitioners, how much credence to give to the PAC construct. It is phenomenological, but not about the individual's unique FRAME OF REFERENCE. It is a generalisation. Different counsellors will have varied feelings about this.

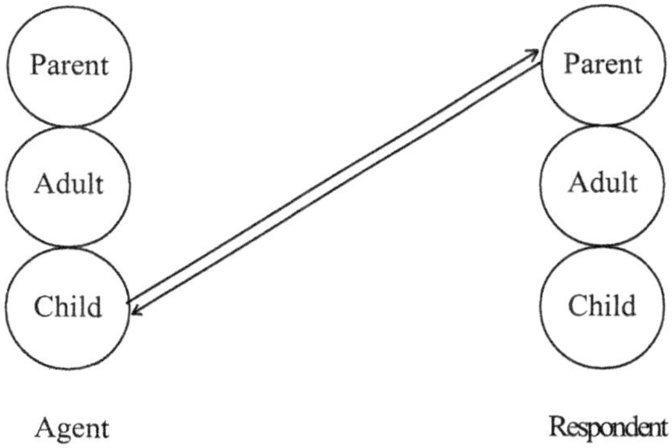


For Berne, the phenomena around thinking, feeling and behaving can be fitted into a number—five or six in the functional version of the model—of EGO STATES. These are patterns which are phenomenologically unique to each individual. My set of experiences around Parent will be very different from other peoples'. These differences exist at a number of levels. My own parents will have given me distinctive experience of parenting. I will have had other parent-like experiences from school teachers, for example. I will have developed an adult dialogue within myself about what parenting should be and might have put that into practice with my own children. There is an element of stereotyping in concepts of ego states. We know what punitive parenting is, even if only from fairy tales. Beneath all of this lies cultural experience. In working with Asian clients, I am aware that what I take to be good parenting and what is taken for good parenting in a more traditional non-Western culture can be very different indeed.

Thus, Berne invites us to fit together personal, family and cultural experiences. EGO STATES are generalisations of individual, phenomenal (perceived) experience. Always, therefore, we need to be alert to the FRAME OF REFERENCE of the client. When I use PAC language, do I mean what the client means? As a generalisation, the three ego states have the following connotations:

*Parent*: Someone who presumes an authority or superiority over another. In real or surrogate parents this can be wholly appropriate and benign, but between adults can feel manipulative, GAME-like or condescending.

*Adult*: An appropriate and GAME-free state, mainly in the here and now. It construes the respondent as an equal. It tends not to impose conditions of worth.

*Child*: In a one-down position in relation to the Parent. This position is characterised by a need to compensate for the power imbalance imposed by the Parent.

The Parent and the Child are best seen as subdivided. The Parent can be either Nurturing or Critical. It is important not to jump to conclusions about the effects of these ego states as INTROJECTIONS. While it is clear that Critical Parent embodies CONDITIONS OF WORTH, so can the Nurturing Parent: you are only loved, if you accept my care.

The Child can usefully be divided into the Free Child and the Adapted Child. Some would add the Rebellious Child. The Free Child is likely to want mischievous, open and loving play. They are, by and large, accepted for who they are. (The Rebellious Child can use this type of behaviour, but from a stance of feeling unaccepted.) The Adapted Child is under pressure from the Critical Parent. She has to adapt her behaviour to match the requirements of the outside world in general and the Critical Parent in particular. The relationship of Critical Parent to Adapted Child is one instance of the INTROJECTION of CONDITIONS OF WORTH. However, let us keep in mind the PHENOMENOLOGICAL principle: we cannot from this language know our client's experience. We need to wait, to listen or even to ask.

Berne's theory gives a generalised overview of the ego state of individuals. This includes thoughts, feelings and behaviours. What is specific to his theory is this: ego states may be conscious or otherwise and can last over time or switch moment by moment, although the latter is the more usual. While these states are different in precise content for each individual, Berne postulates that they represent roles in life with enough coherence to constitute unconscious (or conscious) communication.

If the whole of the human world was made up of Adult communication, it would indeed be a rational, if slightly tedious, place. There would be no sex, since sex at its best is from Free Child. However there would also be no GAMES, in Berne's special sense of the word. Berne observed that communication could happen along any of the possible lines in the above diagram. (The one sketched in describes ongoing communication between the Child of the agent and the Parent of the respondent.) When communication is set between ego states that collude in continuing a pattern, the individuals can feel themselves to be locked into something that feels irrational, which Berne terms a GAME.

In the example below, we can see how GAME-like experiences can influence both the agent and the respondent without either of them being aware of it.

**Illustrative Example**: *Maureen, a high school teacher, is negotiating how she will be involved in next year's English courses with her Head of Department. Maureen sets out throughout their discussion to placate her colleague, without even realising it. It is as if she were dealing with her father again. Throughout her teenage years, her father had given her the message—the CONDITION OF WORTH—that she needed to do anything rather than to cause him to need to be angry with her!*

*Meanwhile, Steve, her colleague, is beginning to feel rather ill at ease with the whole process. On the surface, they are having a reasonable enough conversation. It seems to be going OK. Yet Steve is feeling uncomfortable. He is irritable for no apparent reason. What is it about this conversation? Or about Maureen? He can feel that he is edgy. Is he really such an unreasonable person?*

*Although Steve and Maureen have worked together well over the last two years, Maureen still does not feel at home in her relationship with Steve. She experiences what TA practitioners call 'rubber banding'. She is pulled back to old versions of relationships with authority figures. It is as if part of her is on the alert, a part that might turn out to be a 'bad daughter' configuration.*

*She therefore approaches Steve from Child. This is the pattern of the diagram above. Steve then experiences being dragged unconsciously into Parent. (It is not how he normally is. He is trying to be in Adult. The result is that, unbeknown to either of them, Steve and Maureen are now caught in a GAME, a pattern of communication. Maureen is at one level familiar enough with the apprehension of being a 'bad'—that is, demanding—daughter. Steve, though, feels thrown. He is being pushed into a role he does not normally occupy. Where has he to go?*

Look back to the diagram above. You will notice that the two lines of communication between agent and responder run in parallel to each other. This indicates that the GAME which is afoot is an ongoing one. Neither Steve nor Maureen knows what is happening. Both are equally trapped into a system. What is attractive and useful about this way of thinking is that it can work to dispel blame. Both Steve and Maureen might feel quite sore with the other. Yet, each is helplessly caught into a pattern which they cannot immediately escape. Recognising this gives the option to both of them to escape the blame game.

I am particularly struck, in my work with young adults, by how they often need to think hard about their relationships with parents, but are inhibited from doing this freely by a sense of guilt. Parents can't be attacked, criticised or harmed. Again, here is a rich array of CONDITIONS OF WORTH. TA has the capacity as a language to objectify the patterns of interaction so that, if the client wants, they can be blame-free.

## WORKING WITH MAUREEN: TWO POSSIBILITIES

The essence of work with Maureen is that she has received strong CONDITIONS OF WORTH, mainly from her father, that she must be a compliant daughter. Demanding equals bad. Therefore she has to repress her needs, indeed her ability to feel need as legitimate. This pattern has reproduced itself in her relationship with Steve. Steve is not her father, in that he does not want to be in a conditioned or oppressive relationship. (This of course keeps matters relatively simple. Often, the 'rubber-banding' referred to above in the example is triggered by people who do reproduce some of the qualities of a difficult past relationship.) I want to use my work with Maureen to illustrate two possibilities for using the PAC construct in client work. It is not so much the *what* of the work that matters. It is the *why*. Integration is always about careful and responsible REFLECTIVE PRACTICE.

### Listening to Maureen

Berne's claim that the general concept of, say, 'Child is phenomenological' is based on the fact that it has characteristic behaviours attached to it (the client can locate the sensation of 'being in Child' within her own perceived experience). This set of behaviours points to a discrete part of the self. The Child wants to communicate. This is wholly consistent, I notice, with Dave Mearns' claim that configurations of the self require empathy. In the example of the Nun and the Little Girl ('Elizabeth': Mearns, 1994: 12–14.), the Nun required as much care from the therapist as the more attractive Little Girl. Therefore, there is an aspect of Maureen that wants to be heard but will appear briefly, concealed behind the controlled and frightened Adult of the teacher who finds herself in therapy.

The Child appeared to me as awkward body language, a turning in of the knee, a playing with the hair, a certain sulkiness. Verbally, Maureen would find a whingeing tone to her voice which was not usually there. I could imagine her trying to placate Steve, unconsciously, but with the result that she irritated and frustrated him.

The recognition of the Child must be always tentative and never spoken out of counsellor authority. I hint about what she feels as Child, gently and tentatively. I keep returning to Brian Thorne's word 'tenderness' at moments like these. Some clients will be happy to receive feedback about body language. Others will be thrown off-track, embarrassed, or will take even a passing observation as a shift away from them by the counsellor. There are, again, no rules. The counsellor needs to test the water with care.

There is no need, in this instance, to be explicit about the Bernean construct of Child. All that is needed is that the counsellor can offer empathy towards that part of Maureen which needs reassurance, feels oppressed by Steve's (imagined) imposition of CONDITIONS OF WORTH. She can even be challenged as to whether Steve *really* wants her to be compliant. (Is this consistent with other things she has said?)

In summary, the PAC construct has taught me to see Maureen more clearly, through bodily and verbal behaviour. However, check out that what you *think* you see is, indeed, the client's phenomenon. Test through empathy. If it is a false presupposition, it will return to you unused. There is nothing wrong with learning that you are wrong in understanding a client. It clarifies what there is to be understood and welcomed of the client. Remember that the risk of congruent observation has to be judged in each and every case. Can the client use it therapeutically or is it a barrier? Above all, check that the client does not receive it as either illegitimate power or disapproval. As a male counsellor, I could have been in danger of following Steve down the track of becoming too much like Maureen's father, unless my relationship with her stands on a firm enough foundation.

Irresponsible risks are exactly that; yet, there is no therapy without some risk.

## LEARNING WITH MAUREEN

In the Illustrative Example above, I made it clear that Steve does not have the characteristics of Maureen's father. However, life is not often so helpful. Clients have to deal with those versions of Steve who are oppressive.

This raises a profound question about the nature of counselling. Is its role to help clients survive, or is it concerned with issues of social justice? I strongly believe that therapy is politically engaged (Proctor et al., 2006). Therefore it is a legitimate role of the therapist, with the explicit, informed and emotionally available consent of the client, to share in a learning process with the client. How might this work with Maureen?

From time to time, I offer the client a way of understanding what is going on in a third-party relationship, as a sub-contract of our work together. I explain that there is a particular way of thinking—again, a language—which might help them see what is happening to them, and might help them deal with it differently. This is particularly important in the case of adults being bullied at work, for example.

If the offer is taken up, and that freely rather than because the client feels that the counsellor must be 'obeyed' as the authority figure in the relationship, then the preliminaries of PAC can be taught in ten minutes. (It is part of TA that it sees itself as especially democratic because the client learns the theory as well as the counsellor. However, this line of reasoning does not particularly either help or hinder me.) When I am sure that Maureen has a grasp of the principles, I would then invite her to use these to think through the situation. I am not willing to do that for her. I am not into problem solving, but into facilitating an educative process. I will learn a lot from mistakes or blockages in Maureen's thinking. I will also pay attention to the possibility that she cannot use the concept. (Me! A Child! That's ridiculous. I'm a teacher, for God's sake!) One direct outcome might be that Maureen comes to recognise that she is skewing her relationship with Steve, because she is rubber-banding back to father. Another might be that she comes to recognise that the nature of Steve's intentions towards her is not as sinister as she feels it to be. A third outcome might be that she comes to see real similarities between Steve and her father, and that there is real oppression going on. As the counsellor, I can check, I can challenge, but I cannot decide what is real for Maureen.

As with any insights gained in therapy, the counsellor cannot, of course, guarantee that the outcome is accurate. Maureen might conclude that Steve is very much like her father. I may doubt this. I could not possibly know myself to be right. I cannot save Maureen from making the situation worse. All I can do is to alert her to the uncertainty of her, and my, conclusions.

This second way of using the PAC construct is very different from the first. In the first, PAC merely informed the counsellor, who learned how to see the world through a particular lens. In the second, the concept is taught and is a way of helping the client to understand the world differently. It gives to the client a new level of decision-making. It is riskier.

### ... AND ONE NOT TO USE, PERHAPS

There are risks that I believe to be, in principle, too risky to take. The most obvious relationship to look at would be the one in the counselling room. While occasionally the construct might be a useful way of thinking about the therapeutic relationship within supervision, I am inclined to think that it is too great a risk to refer to what is happening between therapist and client in PAC. There are a number of reasons for this:

1. Because the model involves labels which are not specific to the client, then applying these to the client *in situ* is a tactic which is likely to distort the power dynamic within the room.
2. By extension, the therapist in a difficult moment can use the model interpretatively and defensively against the client (Ellingham, 2005).
3. Because of the nature of the model, one of the roles of the therapist in its use is to check out that what is being put forward actually fits the emotional state for the client. To do this with the immediate relationship would require the therapist to be in two roles at the same time. In just the same way that I speculated, above, that Steve might have difficulties containing Maureen's sense of threat that was projected onto him, so it could be for the therapist in respect of her client.

The relationship is best dealt with in direct and real terms that avoid constructs that may give insight but also make for problems of personal power.

## In conclusion

The PAC construct is a good example of a pattern of thinking about relating which needs to be understood in depth and then used with caution. As ever, the key aim of relating to the client is the relationship itself and not any subsidiary pay-offs.

# 5

# EMBODIED AWARENESS: THE MIND'S MIRROR

> Experience occurs at the boundary between the organism and its environment ... Experience is the function of this boundary, and psychologically what is real are the whole configurations of this functioning, some meaning being achieved, some action completed ... We speak of the organism contacting the environment, but it is the contact that is the simplest and first reality. (Perls, Hefferline & Goodman, 1951/1973: 273)

> Psychological maladjustment exists when the organism denies to awareness significant sensory and visceral experiences, which consequently are not symbolised and organised into the GESTALT of the self-structure. When this situation exists, there is a basic or potential psychological tension. (Proposition XIV, Rogers, 1951: 510)

Carl Rogers proposed that INCONGRUENCE arises when some experiences 'sensory and visceral'—at the core of our bodily existence—are denied to the realm of our symbolic awareness. Typically, for the person whose experiencing of life is distorted by CONDITIONS OF WORTH, they are unable to feel, to know fully, either their own evaluation of a situation or sometimes the positive evaluation of others (good feedback). Carl Rogers and Fritz Perls have much in common, as the quotations above suggest (Greenberg et al., 1993). Perls' genius has been in seeing the process of experiencing as basic to therapy, and being able to describe that process, and its interruptions, with great richness. Like Rogers, he is committed to a PHENOMENOLOGICAL view of therapy: it is the client's individual experience that matters.

GESTALT, particularly as Perls himself practised it, has become, at worst, notorious. Perls was a showman, and clearly enjoyed holding centre stage. Some of his techniques, like the Empty Chair, have been stereotyped as 'the heart of Gestalt'. This is unjust, a distortion of modern GESTALT, particularly that which follows the work of Laura Perls. However, at no point in this chapter do I want to suggest that the person-centred counsellor needs to work in a GESTALT way, and least of all like Fritz Perls himself. The question is: What can we integrate of the theory of awareness Perls puts forward?

## GESTALT THERAPY AND GESTALT PSYCHOLOGY

GESTALT is a German word meaning 'whole', in the sense that a picture may have many parts but comprises one whole image. GESTALT psychologists, who preceded Perls by about fifty years, had already noticed that in human perception the whole is always greater than the sum of the parts. That is to say, when I see a cricket match in the next field, what I see, how my brain puts it together in my consciousness, is a cricket match, and not twenty-two men in whites with six sticks, two bats and a ball. I see the whole partly because it is the whole that represents meaning. I can ask what to do with a ball and a stick, but as long as I know about cricket I cannot intelligently ask what to do with a cricket match.

An early GESTALT psychologist, Bluma Zeigarnik (1900–1988), noted that humans have an innate need to complete patterns. (This has great survival benefit. In order to hunt efficiently, we need to intuit patterns and movement very quickly.) Thus, if we hear the first four notes of the British National Anthem—presuming we are very familiar with it—it is almost impossible not to complete the rest of the musical phrase, at least in our heads. Using these insights of GESTALT psychology, Perls postulates that distress comes from a failure to complete patterns of experience, which he calls figures. Figures are set against the background of life. This is the FIGURE AND GROUND motif. Incomplete figures prevent people from 'getting closure' and moving on. We get stuck. Characteristically we get stuck in past 'unfinished business'. (GESTALT has contributed two or three well-known bits of jargon to popular psychology!) We get stuck by a process of the denial of current awareness to ourselves. Perls had two memorable dicta to cover aspects of this theory:

1. Loose your mind and come to your senses.
2. Not why but how: not then but now.

GESTALT therapy has a great commitment to leading the client into a living in the present moment.

## Gestalt THEORY OF EXPERIENCE: KEY POINTS

To become a GESTALT therapist requires two to four years of training. It cannot be done by reading. Those person-centred trained counsellors who believe differently, and are being seduced by another approach, are acting dangerously. To become a Gestaltist, invest in the training, if that is what you want. However, a programme of reading can help in an understanding of the principles of this discipline. An excellent first level reader is Harris (2003). For an intermediate text, I find Sills, Fish and Lapworth (1995) has clarity and feels well lived in. Finally the authority on GESTALT therapy theory remains Perls, Hefferline & Goodman (1951/1973), a tough read but an exhaustive account. A sophisticated comparison of Perls' and Rogers' thought can be found in the first section of Greenberg, Rice & Elliott (1993). See also Worsley (2002), Chapter 13.

However, for the purposes of this chapter, the relevant theory can be stated very briefly:

- 'In GESTALT therapy, *the only goal is awareness*' (Yontef & Simkin, 1989: 337, original italics). The reason for this is that awareness constitutes contact between the organism and its environment. This exactly parallels Rogers' notion of contact: Condition One, Rogers, 1957. However Perls also sees this contact as the place that meaning evolves, which parallels Eugene Gendlin's 1962/1997 work on felt-meaning.
- There are three zones of awareness. The *inner zone* is our awareness of our own bodies, sometimes called proprioception. The *outer zone* is what we experience of the outer world through the five senses. The *middle zone* is that

part of our awareness that is made up of fantasies, INTROJECTS and the like, our mental life.

- Awareness, in quite a concrete, physical and bodily sense, is the mirror of the mind, both a source and an indicator of personal, mental well-being.
- Experiences stand out. They emerge as a figure against a (back)ground. Each figure needs to be vibrant and complete, if we are to experience well-being. (The Zeigarnik effect, an innate need to complete patterns, see above.)
- We INTROJECT rules, messages or models presented to the organism from outside itself. (Here Perls is much like Rogers. However, Rogers stresses the conditional nature of the INTROJECT—you are only loved, *if*… —whereas Perls stresses the *external* nature of the message. Even so, they are close to each other, for this difference is merely a matter of emphasis.)
- INTROJECTS interrupt our experiencing. When this happens, we get stuck. There is unfinished business.
- Getting stuck can sometimes involve being stuck in the past—not then, but now—or getting stuck in the head—not why but how.
- Getting stuck is a matter of choice, and often involves a stuck use of language. The client will often say: 'I can't do this.' The GESTALT therapist might invite her to replace this with: 'I won't do this.'
- The key point of it all for me is the relationship between REFLEXIVITY and SPONTANEITY. I have argued elsewhere (Worsley, 2002: 125–7) that well-being involves a balance between living spontaneously in the here and now, without being stuck in the head, and living REFLEXIVELY, so that our awareness is available to us. Perls is clear that we can become more aware of our level of awareness, and that this can be a healing manoeuvre.
- Experience is interrupted by avoidance.
- An experience (the figure set clearly against its ground) consists of a number of stages of initiation, arousal, satisfaction and completion. This is called the GESTALT cycle of experience.
- Between each cycle of experience is a period of repose, which

Perls refers to as the futile or fertile void. No cycle completes without entering this void. I speculate that this is not just a matter of concrete experiencing of repose. It also involves the existential anxiety of facing many voids. See 'Migrants' in Chapter 9, below.

### WORKING WITH ALISTAIR

Alistair is a very competent pianist. Towards the end of his work with me, he told me that at those times when he felt a low-level, gnawing depression, he was unable to play the piano. I think that I would have taken scant note of this, taking it for granted as typical of depression. However, Alistair was keen to work on this. He felt increasingly that it stood for something important. I thought again of Rogers' words:

> Internal communication is clear with feelings and symbols well matched. (Rogers, 1961/1967: 154)

Alistair's persistent fascination in the figure of 'not playing the piano' suggested to me that his process was striving to symbolise a need to grasp an aspect of his own experience of being depressed. I am truly intrigued, and often moved, by clients' ability to know, at the edge of their awareness, what their own needs are and to strive to fulfil them. Alistair sought meaning in an experience which he clearly felt to be an embodiment of ... but of what? We both needed to spend time being puzzled.

I asked Alistair to imagine what it is like to try and play while feeling depressed. I had no sense of him simply feeling too down to bother. Not playing felt active. He was interrupting himself from taking up an otherwise pleasurable activity. As I imagined him playing, I reflected to him my awareness that he approached much of his music as well-crafted, beautiful, but with occasional pleasure in the cacophonous. The latter he could relate to anger or rebellion. When he was depressed, he had trouble accessing his anger. This is not surprising, but it is not the full story.

The notion of well-crafted beauty threw him back to talking of his childhood. All the while this seemed to me connected to the physiological experience of interruption. His parental home was 'loving, God-fearing but not prone to joy'. Well-crafted beauty would not be welcomed there. There was a puritanical harshness to that environment.

The image or symbol of not playing the piano, he explained to me, seemed to be about how difficult it is to feel well-crafted beauty when depressed. This, in turn, resonated with his lack of motivation to take care of himself at such times, and inversely with his new-found ability to assert his practical need for self-care in his current work and his family life.

When Alistair is depressed, it is not that he does not play the piano. He interrupts his desire to play, in order to symbolise his lack of willingness to care for himself. He mobilises his musical self and then blocks any acting upon it. Far from being lethargic, muscularly slack, he is tense, blocking, self-withholding.

The next stage of his work was to return to his increased felt-need to care for himself. For Alistair, this meant claiming a mental right to space for himself, and implementing this self-consciously through work-a-day strategies of time management.

Healthy living is for Perls about making good contact with the environment. This enables us to complete experiential Gestalts just as the organism needs:

> From the point of view of psychotherapy, when there is good contact—e.g. a clear, bright figure freely energized from an empty background—then there is no peculiar problem concerning the relations of 'mind' and 'body' or 'self' and 'external world'. (Perls, Hefferline & Goodman, 1951/1973: 303)

When Alistair played the piano fluently, that act was, for him, a bright figure. The background receded. It was (re)creation. He was renewed as his playing refreshed him from that which he could relegate to the dull greyness of the margins of awareness. When he blocked this playing, far from seeming apathetic, he was tense and self-denying:

> ... we have here the typical picture of neurosis: under-aware proprioception and finally perception, and hypertonus of deliberateness and muscularity. (Yet let us insist again that this

> condition is not unfunctional, in the given chronic low-grade emergency ... (Perls, Hefferline & Goodman, 1951/1973: 313)

Perls makes two points here. The first is that, under what he terms neurotic stress, a person will be unduly unaware of the inner zone, and will not perceive, and therefore understand, this lack of awareness. This is accompanied by stiffness of action and muscular tension. (Alistair was too tense to be merely apathetic.)

However, Perls also makes the point that this condition is not a DYSFUNCTION in the sense of a meaningless going-wrong of awareness. It carries other information. If Alistair had been in danger, then this focus upon a tense being and a resistance to playing would have been appropriate. He was interrupting his playing just because he felt a danger that existed, not in the outer zone, the material world, but within his middle zone. He interrupted himself just when he was most keenly aware of the lack of self-care he had, and associated with his birth-home.

As we complete each GESTALT of our experiencing, we permit ourselves to move through a cycle of experience without undue interruption. This cycle Alistair was denying to himself. In becoming aware, in a bodily sense, of what he was doing, Alistair experienced an inner shift at two separate levels:

1. He could experience himself reflexively. That is, he could feel the tense muscular blocking, and know it for what it was, an interruption to his self-caring and the remnants of the denial of self-love within his birth family. This increased awareness would likely have been therapeutic in itself.
2. However, Alistair could also develop a conscious attitude towards this, and thence to seek for a new way of being aware. He linked it back to his birth family and the lack of joy. This interpretation of the muscular stiffness belonged to him; it was through an active, shared, PHENOMENOLOGICAL exploration of what it felt like not to play the piano that the meaning of it emerged for him.

## Discussion

My work with Alistair was marked by that fact that he, rather than I, spotted that not-playing-the-piano was full of meaning. At first glance I had taken it as just a fairly predictable symptom of depression, a version of lassitude. However, he kept bringing us back to it. I felt, on reflection, struck by this insistence as an expression of his ACTUALISING TENDENCY. He was already aware at the level of felt-meaning (Gendlin, 1962 /1997), at gut level, that this was important. What remained was to discover why it mattered.

It seems to me that part of empathy is very often to slow down the experiencing pattern of the client. Whenever I try to understand a client by listening, by responding, by checking out, then what it is that the client is experiencing is slowed down. It is brought into conscious focus. It unfolds before us. This happens with most empathic activities. All that is different about these moments with Alistair is that I needed to ask, negotiate with him, a slowing down so that his experience, past and present, could have room to puzzle us for a while.

The story could feasibly have been different. It could easily have been the case that I became interested in Alistair's not-playing-the-piano, and that he could have been resistant to thinking about it. I am happy to suggest an exploration of aspects of the client that neither of us sees clearly. If the client resists, then it is not my job to force the issue. To be willing to explore feelings or behaviour that is not yet understood is an exact parallel to Dave Mearns' openness to empathise with all aspects of the client. (See Chapter 3.) Empathy beyond the client's conscious knowing carries with it a certain risk; but then so does failure to empathise!

Fritz Perls offers a pattern for understanding the nature of human experience which provides a lens through which to strive to understand the client. The client's FRAME OF REFERENCE is not just what she knows she feels. For that is to contradict the concept that our feelings, thinking and knowing is often EMBODIED long before it is symbolised.

It is useful that Perls' theory is so close to that of Rogers, and in particular of Gendlin. However, even if this were not the case, it would not block the usefulness of the theory. It might make its integration a more difficult task. All lenses can be of use. All lenses have some degree of unavoidable and natural distortion.

## CONCLUSION

The theory of GESTALT therapy provides me with, provokes me towards, a clearer and fuller understanding of the nature of awareness, not least in its intimate relationship to the body as a felt and lived entity. Without some wrestling with the work of Fritz and Laura Perls, my understanding of Alistair's not-playing-the-piano would have been poorer.

I note that this understanding required of me a minimal sort of directiveness, a saying to Alistair: Can we please pause and think harder about what you are experiencing. Where? How? When? However, this sits quite happily in a relationship which is essentially and in principle non-directive. Whenever I offer an empathic response, in effect I give the same message: Can we pause and think and feel this more slowly and perhaps more clearly?

There is no need to venture into elements of GESTALT practice which may be deeply seductive, offering the frustrated or unconfident therapist tools, powers and performance potential. Those GESTALT therapists whom I have worked with have also spotted these potentials for seduction. By and large, with one exception, they too have resisted the seducer.

# 6

# COUNSELLING AS DIALOGUE: WORKING WITH MEANING IN THERAPY

> The central paradox is that this [the existential Self] is our most private place, which we also yearn to share. I have grown into the habit of capitalising 'Self' ... to emphasise the sheer magnitude, complexity, uniqueness and beauty of the concept. (Dave Mearns, in Mearns & Thorne, 2000: 57)

> If we take the Person-Centered Approach (PCA) seriously as a *client*-centered approach, we have to go back to our clients in order to engage them in an individualized, shared process of encounter and reflection ... From a dialogical point of view, therapists and clients are not only seen as being *in* relationships; as persons they *are* relationships, which makes them different in each therapeutic contact. (Schmid, 2005: 75)

Above, Dave Mearns stresses that being a Self is complex, unique and beautiful. Peter Schmid, complementing him, sees the uniqueness of each person as being in their encounters with others. Each encounter is unique. The DIALOGUE between people in which encounters are rooted is similarly special and particular to each relationship. There can be no stereotyping of meetings. Each is simply itself. It is in this that I believe Irvin Yalom to be right in saying that we need to invent afresh the therapy for each client (Yalom, 2001, Chapter 10). This chapter aims to explore what can be integrated into the person-centred relationship in the name of human encounter.

This is without doubt the most difficult chapter in this book. I do not apologise for that. There is only space to hint at what is a huge field to reflect upon. Yet, for me, it has become the most important of the areas to think about. The question posed here goes beyond the integration of theory in a formal sense. In the previous three chapters, I have been able to point to specific concepts from the person-centred approach, transactional analysis and GESTALT, and then illustrate and discuss how taking these seriously would impact upon the therapeutic process. This chapter, by contrast, looks at a number of ways of thinking about relating itself.

I will look at what Peter Schmid means by encounter. I will look at the contribution of EXISTENTIAL thinking to encounter. Lastly, I will look at the contribution of two Jewish thinkers to our understanding of meeting each other at depth: Martin Buber and Emmanuel Levinas. I want to acknowledge that a cogent account of encounter at depth is put forward in Mearns and Cooper (2005). Their approach differs from mine, but is a good next step beyond this chapter.

Understanding encounter involves a venture into some philosophy. This might feel at first sight very off-putting. Do not let yourself be deskilled. It is not difficult in the way you may fear. Often we can be overcome with the apprehension that we will not understand (and that, of course, others will), as if what was to be understood was just hard facts. Memories arise of not following a maths lesson at school. Do not be fooled. This is not about head-understanding. It is about imagination. If I can be seized by an idea put forward by Peter Schmid or Martin Buber, I can be deeply puzzled by it until something in my imagination fires.

When I really strive to relate to someone else, I find that I sometimes do rather strange, IDIOSYNCRATIC things, which seem both risky and yet deeply trustworthy:

**Illustrative example**: *Alan was a shy man in his early forties. I met him in his doctor's surgery. He was deeply depressed. The depression was the tip of the iceberg. He was a librarian who lived with his aged mother. He had few, if any, close relationships. He was lonely and believed himself to be unlovely and inadequate as a person. In our relating, I was struck by his loveliness, in spite of himself. After a number of weeks, with some progress made, I reflected to him his isolation and his aloneness. He could not imagine anyone wanting to like him. I had heard a couple of weeks previously that he had tried a poetry group. (He was afraid of those who went*

> *there.) I asked him which poets he enjoyed. As a Welshman, he particularly enjoyed David Jones (in Latin) and R.S. Thomas. I share his love of Thomas. (See Chapter 9.) We talked about reading Thomas together. There is bleakness and hope there. I enjoyed this. I enjoyed him. It felt a little self-indulgent. Yet, together we were good company. It was actual and genuine. Healing has many forms. We were in relationship. That was all. And the poetry too was part of each of us. I could trust him with this intimacy.*

## ENCOUNTER

> I risk myself … I let myself go into the immediacy of the relationship … In these moments, there is, to borrow Buber's phrase, a real 'I–Thou' relationship, a timeless living in the experience which is between the client and me. It is at the opposite pole from seeing the client, or myself, as an object. (Rogers, 1955: 268ff., original emphases, cited by Schmid, 1998: 79–80)

Peter Schmid (1998: 79) describes the notion of relationship as encounter emerging only slowly in the thought of Carl Rogers. He ascribes particular importance to Rogers' experience of working with PSYCHOTIC people in the WISCONSIN PROJECT, and to his meeting with Martin Buber, the Jewish philosopher of relationship. Schmid is particular fond of pointing out that, in a number of European languages, including English, the word encounter can be divided in two: En-Counter. This could be rendered as In-Contra in Latin. We are both In and Contra: over against. We are face to face rather than side by side. Images of encounter are different from images of accompanying. The basic rationale for encounter is that person-centred counselling is about helping the other person (or rather helping each other) become a person more fully. We thus bring all of who we are to that En-Counter.

I want to note a small number of points from Schmid (2005) particularly:

- 'Person-specific is not symptom-specific … or disorder-specific, and not at all disorder-oriented, but instead is uniquely process-specific … As part of the relationship, the therapist is different, if the client is different' (Schmid, 2005: 79–80). In other words, person-centred counsellors work not with 'illnesses' but with people who are unique. Therefore in any relationship we respond in unique and IDIOSYNCRATIC ways. (See my Illustrative Example above.) It is one of my critiques of CLASSICAL CLIENT-CENTRED therapists that some do not allow themselves the freedom to respond. We need in encounter to have this freedom. The art form is to combine responsiveness with reliability.

- Schmid describes encounter as a Thou–I relationship, in that the counsellor awaits what the client will disclose and reveal of themselves, (as opposed to: What do I see over there?). I want to add to this: How do I respond from within me to what is disclosed? I am grateful to Pete Sanders for his observation that, in this work, it is the counsellor's self-awareness within that is the key. What is actually *done* in the room may appear on the surface, on video for instance, to be the same. How can this be? Not only does *what I do* get communicated. Sometimes, just *who I am* is what the client perceives, sometimes in full awareness and sometimes not.
- Within an encounter, the partners seek for knowledge, but it is what Schmid calls *existential knowledge*. That is, it is based on experiencing and on the context of the relationship itself.

**Illustrative example**: *Terrence worked in a call centre as a computer technician. In his spare time he was fascinated by programming. His job no doubt was unfulfilling, and he was worthy of better. He had been chronically unwell. As I listened to him, I became aware that I wanted to treat him as a hypochondriac, but without good reason. It was simply that his illness infected the therapy hour. I reeled from it, nauseous with boredom. Gradually I realised how his world was impoverished. He ate, slept, worked, paid his bills and was alone. In a sense the illness was all that rendered him interesting, and even that was scarcely a success with me or with the girls! Ten years ago, I would have backed away from clients like Terrence.*

*Finally, I took a deep breath, and offered him the observation. 'You are just so alone in life. Stranded. And you make sure you keep it like that. And it hurts.' There was a pained silence. If I had hit the nail on the head, it had certainly brought no comfort. Yet, at least here was a painful place to begin. Could Terrence relate to me?*

Schmid's thinking about encounter has led us to see relating as about the uniqueness of the responses which both client and counsellor can make, as well as the counsellor's need to respond from within herself at a deep and personal level. These two points are not difficult to understand on the surface, although they are tough to put into practice. However, the final point about existential knowledge is not at all easy, and yet it is crucial. Why do I call my comments to Terrence, above, existential?

My comments to Terrence could be seen as either merely empathic—this is how it feels?—or even as somewhat diagnostic—this is what you do, you know!—if it were not for the words 'and you make sure you keep it like that'. I point to, show my understanding of, Terrence's deep way of being. He chooses to preserve his isolation because the alternative is too scary for him. Existence is the way we stand out in the universe and it involves choice. We cannot renounce our responsibility for that. At the point that I spoke, Terrence chose isolation. I suggested, in making my observation, that this choice was neither necessary nor healthy.

That it is not necessary is a matter of fact; people can change. That it is not healthy is a far more subversive comment than it seems. I *am* saying that there are 'right' ways to live. I am not merely making a mental health observation, such as that taking heroin messes with your head. I am saying that to live is essentially to make choices, and that to refuse these is—inauthentic or what?[1]

I think this is a controversial thing to say: we have choices about ways of being, and we are morally bound to make them unless we fall into a position that lacks integrity. I want to ask of

1. But see Adorno, 2003, who makes a good case that the word 'authentic' is just a tribal word about conformity.

this position three questions: Is it directive? Is it in accord with Rogers' thinking? Where does it leave us?

It is directive, because it means that, at some level, the counsellor holds an agenda for what it is to be human.

Yet, it is at the heart of Rogers' thinking. Person-centred therapy can be stereotyped as West Coast of America, 1960s amoral liberalism. This is not the case. For instance, we consistently implement the CORE CONDITIONS, not just because they are therapeutically useful, but because they are ethically essential (Schmid, 1998: 86). To fail to do so is immoral. Proctor et al. (2006) have just put forward a similar argument positing that to ignore the political consequences of being person-centred is also wrong. Rogers entered into a dialogue with the theologian, Paul Tillich, on 7th March 1965. In sketching out their common ground around self-affirmation, Rogers observed, 'I also liked your phrase about the antimoral act being one that contradicts the self-realization of the individual' (Kirschenbaum & Henderson, 1990b: 66). We are, Rogers believes, morally obliged to offer to the other person that which will promote her self-realisation. The EXISTENTIAL intervention is person-centred because to be person-centred is indeed to hold an agenda for being human, and an ethic which prohibits running counter to this.

Where does this leave us? We need to work out what it is, essentially, to exist. This is not at all obvious or free of controversy. We will need the help of EXISTENTIAL PHILOSOPHY to see even what the options are. Yet, the cornerstone of encounter turns out to be that the counsellor must be willing to engage in the DIALOGUE of existing with her client. EXISTENTIALISM will help to clarify what this might mean.

## EXISTENTIALISM[2]

Professor John Macquarrie notes that existentialists show a wide range of beliefs and methods. They seem to have little in common

2. Please see the Appendix: Resources for Learning for a list of books that will take you beyond the scope of this chapter.

in terms of shared ideas. Therefore what marks out existentialism is its shared style of philosophising. He continues:

> It is the philosophy of the subject rather than the object ... [F]or the existentialist the subject is the existent in the whole range of its existing. He is not only a thinking subject but an initiator of action and a centre of feeling. It is the whole spectrum of existence, known directly and concretely in the very act of existing, that existentialism tries to express. (Macquarrie, 1972: 14–15)

'Existence' is, then, a word with a special meaning. We sometimes speak of *merely* existing as opposed to being fully alive. It is the very opposite of this. In philosophy, existence is the quality of being which is uniquely human. We stand out in the world as subjects, who think, feel and act.

The lighter meaning of this word is already part of the thought of Carl Rogers. He notes that as clients become more functional, more CONGRUENT, they increase in 'the existential quality of satisfying living' (Rogers, 1961/1967b: 163). This satisfaction is based upon a number of qualities. We move away from façades, 'oughts', meeting expectations and pleasing others; we move towards self-direction and being-in-process; we increase in complexity and openness to experience; we accept self and others. If existence is a standing out, then, Rogers claims, to be open to our own ORGANISMIC VALUING PROCESS is what he terms THE GOOD LIFE, existential living.

All existentialists are united by their interest in humans as subjects of experience, but they are divided into many camps by their differing beliefs about what it is that is truly human. The key word here is 'authenticity'. A characteristic claim of many existentialists is that we must live authentically. In Sartre's terms, we must avoid 'bad faith', which is to live by hiding in roles. What is authenticity?

If there is a common theme here, it is that life is difficult, at times unpleasant. It is not authentic to avoid this, particularly by deceiving oneself in the process. I therefore enjoy Mick Cooper's tongue-in-cheek description of existential therapy as 'similar to person-centred therapy ... only more miserable!' (Cooper, 2003: 1).

EXISTENTIAL philosophers, and some but by no means all existential therapists, have a vested interest in encouraging their clients to live in a particular way.

At the very least, person-centred counsellors need to hold within themselves the questions which clients have to face in order to live authentically. These include, from Yalom (1980):

- Facing the anxiety (ANGST) that death is inevitable but mysterious and perhaps deeply threatening.
- Facing the fact that we are responsible for our own lives and cannot, with integrity, escape that fact. As such we are committed to *will* that which we decide for. Much depression, for example, can be seen as an escape from *willing* the future.
- Facing the fact that, despite our best efforts, we can be stranded in isolation. Even if we can manage to live in company, of necessity we die alone.
- Life does not bring with it inherent meaning. We need to develop our own meaning. Thus, meaninglessness and all that goes with this, is a constant threat.

In face of the first of these threats, Yalom observes:

> The fear of death always percolates beneath the surface … Death is a visitor in every course of therapy. To ignore its presence is to give the message that it is too terrible to discuss. (Yalom, 2002: 124)

Therefore, at the level of personal development, the therapist must be available to discuss that which creates deep, EXISTENTIAL anxiety. The stress of this is that the EXISTENTIAL themes are universal. We may believe that we are not depressed. Depression belongs to others. (And this is a lie too.) But we cannot say the same of mortality.

However, the structure of existential concerns means that they hover below the surface. We must be prepared to recognise them when the client offers them. We must also be prepared to recognise them when the client denies them, ignores them or flees from them. There can be many patient hours of waiting upon the client, but no therapist can presume that they can escape those moments like the one with Terrence, above, when the truth must be reflected.

It is a scandal, but there is no escape.

> **Illustrative example**: *Emma is a University lecturer in her late twenties. For years she has wrestled with depression. At first she had seen herself as 'bad' on the grounds that she afflicted her depressed self upon her family. In fact, her whole family were either male, and unable to process emotions, or female and depressed. This pattern convinced her of nothing! Her self-deprecation was overwhelming, and is still clearly present. She teaches English, with a particular interest in mediaeval and renaissance work. Part of her fear of herself, and of condemnation, was her fear of texts about hell or demons. Teaching* Paradise Lost *was always difficult. One day, I commented, very much off the top of my head, that I was surprised that she had chosen medieval literature. She looked back at me with certainty. She preferred the risk of Milton to the sterility of Samuel Beckett! Already, years ago, she had made the existential choice for courage. She contacted her depression, even at its darkest, as having some sense of meaning. In Tillich's terms, it is better for her to fear condemnation than live vacuously in the mere present.*

Emma was for me a very important client whom I have, with her permission, written about at some length (Worsley & Joseph, 2007). Her family pattern had rendered her terrified to live. She was at times deeply depressed. Her religious sensibility expressed this often as a fear of condemnation and of hell-fire. Yet, this discussion of literature unveiled for us both the fact that, some years previously, she had taken the decision, deep within herself, that it was better to be truly alive and fearful than to be in a Beckett-like state of emotional paralysis.

To be open to the EXISTENTIAL is a necessary condition of hearing what Emma had within her.

Paul Tillich brings to the EXISTENTIALISM debate a different set of issues, and with a fascinating structure to them. He believed that EXISTENTIAL issues were to be paired off, such that a relative issue always concealed an issue of ultimate concern. Below are paired his relative and ultimate issues:

- Fate, or a sense that life has hidden, impersonal direction which denies personal responsibility, conceals ANGST about death and mortality, in which no being or responsibility remain.

- A sense of personal, physical emptiness, or the emptiness of one's life, conceals an ANGST that life is completely without meaning, and that all is empty, hollow.
- Guilt, or a false sense of moral responsibility for wrong, covers over an ANGST that condemnation is utter and complete. This does not need someone who condemns beyond the self. It does not presuppose a religious or even authoritarian world-view.

For Tillich, the ultimate question is whether we should finally despair. For Emma, however depressed, guilty, self-deprecating she was, she had decided, without knowing it, to suffer rather than despair, even though life could feel to be always on the cusp of despair.

These and other EXISTENTIAL issues are part of the life of clients, not because they are DYSFUNCTIONAL, but because they are human. If they are part of being alive, then they are also challenges to the therapist. Counsellors cannot allow themselves to be deaf to these issues.

## IMAGINATION, STRETCHING OUT

> The existence of I and the speaking of I are one and the same thing. (Buber, 1958: 16)

EXISTENTIAL issues still allow me to remain distant and objective. I can think about death and mortality. I even fool myself that I am in touch with my own anxieties about it, and yet remain safe. If this is what I do, then existential awareness is an enemy to encounter. To encounter another human being, I have found that two Jewish thinkers have been of huge assistance to me: Martin Buber and Emmanuel Levinas. In this very brief space, I will put forward the bare bones of one idea from each of them, and then describe why these seem useful.

**I–Thou**

Reading Buber is not easy. He is a poet as well as a philosopher. Yet, his key concept is not difficult. Let us begin with the opening words of the book:

> To Man the world is twofold, in accordance with his two-fold attitude. The attitude of Man is twofold, in accordance with the twofold nature of the primary words which he speaks. (Buber, 1958: 15)

These opening words of *I and Thou* have, tucked within their dense structure, the roots of Buber's whole approach to human existence. The heart of being human is in relating. We see the world as twofold—other people and objects. That is the basis of our existing. There is nothing more 'real' than our own attitudes which define our construing of the world. I am, because of my basic attitude to the world. I come into being because first I 'see' the world in a particular way. I 'see' it thus by using two primary words: I–Thou and I–It. Buber uses the idea of a primary word to mark up the fact that the I–Thou is not a joining together of two, pre-existing entities, but rather that in the I–Thou relationship that the individual comes to be. It is primary. When I say I–Thou, I relate with my whole being to the other who also shares in the wholeness of being. I intuit the humanness of others. When I say I–It, I construe the other as an object, a *thing*.

The 'saying' of I–Thou can be a silent attitude, not necessarily a literal speaking. This attitude defines our being. We exist, because always we may meet the other as Thou. We become, because we develop over against the other when we first say Thou.

Buber invites us to an act of imagination. Just as Peter Schmid observed above that the client is not a What-over-there, but is a Being-revealed-before-me, so Buber invites me to struggle with the fact that the client is not an object, an It, but is a person in just the same way that I am. Yet, these words are too everyday. They can be taken for granted. Of all of Buber's images that try to shatter this taken-for-granted quality, the one that appeals to me most is in these words:

> Desire itself is transformed 'as it plunges out of its dream into the appearance.' (Buber, 1958: 25)

These last words go far to unlock the key of Buber's thinking. When I desire, I image forth to myself the object of my desire—a girl, a promotion, a bottle of wine, whatever. It is as if my desire dreams in the I–It. Yet, within the I–Thou, I desire the other with a directness that, for the time being, stops me from objectifying what I desire, for in the I–Thou, the other is part of the primacy of being with the I. I can feel a closeness to another, to Thou, which is forgetful of all but the immediacy of relating. Meeting is direct. It blesses. It is of the spaceless, timeless present.

Buber invites me to find the Thou-ness of the other in an act of desire, or *agape*, of soul-love, that is so immediate that I can no longer treat the other as just an object.

**The (absolute) Other**

The philosophy of Emmanuel Levinas is far more complex and elusive than that of Buber. Yet, a single notion from Levinas (1969) is possible to capture. He argues, that in the whole of Western thought, we tend to reduce everything to what he calls the Same, and so we miss its absolute Otherness. This is not about the other person being a Thou, someone like me rather than an object. It is about the fact that the other person is radically Other, and so unknowable. (If this last sentence seems not to make sense, it is not that you do not understand it in the normal sense. It is because it needs to break through to an intuitive sense of 'radically Other'.) People are, finally, mysteries, and need to be (not-) understood like this.

An everyday example of what Levinas means is at the heart of person-centred counselling. When I strive to empathise, I strive to see the world from the other person's point of view. Of course, this is valuable for the most part. Yet there is a problem. It is *me* that is doing this seeing. I do not actually see from the Other. I see from myself. This is a problem that Thomas Nagel (1979) pointed to when he asked: What is it like to be a bat? He answered that when we think we know, we are wrong, because the best the imagination can do is to guess what it is like for Richard to be a bat. But that is so different from what it is for a bat to be a bat. (Nagel answered that it is actually like nothing. For a bat to be a bat is unique. It is Otherness, infinite, unattainable). When I empathise, I tend to reduce everything to the Same, to Richard-like experience. Thus, it is not a matter of inaccuracy that I cannot finally know what an experience is for you. It is that, in not being you, I am radically incapable of getting it right completely.

Therefore, Levinas invites us to hold in our imagination the fact that others are nothing like us at all: totally Other. In relating, we stretch out to the Other in them. It is because they are wholly Other that we cannot own or possess them. Thus they have a prior moral call upon us.

Even more than Buber's concept, Levinas' idea can seem strange, vague, infuriating. Why is it useful?

### Stretching out

The Oxford scholar JL Austin (1961) pointed out that we speak some words not to point to things but to accomplish acts. When I say: With this ring, I marry you, I am not pointing to marrying. I am *doing* it.

When we use the words Thou or Other, within us—not by speaking otherwise than to ourselves—then we stretch out for two of the most crucial aspects of another person. In doing this, we change our attitude, what we do based on how we stand. This has emotional, intellectual, moral and intentional dimensions.

Person-centred counselling is always a matter of attitude.

## Conclusion

I end this chapter with a question. If your client's life lacks meaning, what can you offer? The beginning of EXISTENTIAL encounter may be to not know the answer to this question. Yet, I can only work with someone who is suicidal if I know why I want to be alive. My answers are not relevant *as answers* for my client. However, that I know and love my answers seems to give her hope.

# 7

# AN INTEGRATIVE COUNSELLING TRANSCRIPT

There are no typical moments in integrative, person-centred therapy. To look for a particular, typical moment would be to reduce counselling to a set of formulae. To be integrative is to be open, spontaneous and yet responsible. Even after many years' practice, I am glad to say I am still surprised by what I say to clients at times. Always, the important question is: Was that therapeutic? Often only the client can tell me. I am trying to respond to the client *as she is*.

In the transcript which follows, you will see a few minutes in my work with Helen. I respond in a way that feels unusual and a bit risky. My aim is to engage with Helen with empathy for the way she processes life in the daily world. In Helen's case, this is a matter of respecting her preference for problem solving. Because of the importance of what happens inside me, I have set out the transcript in column one, and next to it have put, in column two, a commentary on what I was feeling and thinking, and what issues this raises.

## Working with Helen

Helen came to work with me through at a small, voluntary agency which uses a mixture of trainee and qualified counsellors. Helen is a fairly newly appointed research and development manager for a telecommunications company. She has a Master's degree in computer science. She presents as smart and efficient. I like her. There is a preciseness to Helen's thinking which feels a little constricted to me. She thinks very logically and needs to have matters put to her with clarity. I can associate this in my own mind with the qualities needed to do degrees in mathematics and computer science.

Helen had been suffering from pressure in her new job, and was depressed. The pressure to perform to schedule was real enough. However, she normally enjoyed tightly scheduled and challenging activities. She was puzzled by her depression.

In the first three sessions, Helen and I have had to work hard so that she recognises that I cannot provide her with any answers or 'magic' exercises that will cure her depression. In session four she has talked about the conflict between her own desire to pursue one line of research and her line manager's need for her to pay attention, for most of her time, to the work of the team he runs. In the second half of the session, she returns to talking about her father, who she first chose to mention in session two.

## Transcript

| Interview | Comments |
|---|---|
| H1: My parents were really very open. I guess I had a privileged and happy childhood. | |
| R1: Mmm. Home was a good place to be. | R1 and R2: This is empathic responding. I want to follow my client, but I also want to engage with her as closely as possible. |
| H2: Yes, but my dad really had a temper. He could be very difficult at times, both for mum and me. | |
| R2: And you struggled with his temper. It was upsetting when he got so angry, I guess. | |
| H3: Yes, and, well its daft but the penny has only just dropped, but he was very much like Gerald (Helen's line manager). | |
| R3: And you're thinking, when you look back, these two men seem pretty similar. (Pause) … and you're wondering if there is any | R3. I notice inside myself that it would be too easy to treat this as a straight TRANSFERENCE: Gerald is another version of Dad. So I very carefully word this to emphasise that the likeness is what *Helen* |

thing in this.

H4: It's funny, really ... the classic old thing ... (pause). I'm thinking that I might struggle with Gerald just like I did with Dad.

R4: When you look back on it, they seem pretty similar to you.

H5: Very much alike. (Helen's face looks suddenly quite panicky.)

R5: Sometimes, you feel really scared of Gerald. Its like, if I don't please him it's a disaster! And that's really scary.

H6: Yes. I know I do that.

R6: And you look quite scared even thinking about it.

H7: Do I? That feels silly.

R7: Helen, I wonder if you can just let yourself *feel* how it is to be scared of Gerald. (Pause. Helen looks very uncomfortable.) Where do you feel the scaredness?

H8: Right here. In my throat. It's like a stone stuck there. I can't speak for it.

R8: When you feel scared, it's like you can't speak. Your throat feels tight, so tight.

H9: Yes. Yes. I can't say anything.

R9: You can't say anything to Gerald. It's just too scary.

spots. This is the PHENOMENOLOGICAL principle. (Then, in spite of my best intentions, I find later—H25 and R25—that I have been fully sucked in by my own thinking of TRANSFERENCE.)

H5: Helen's body language is important. I respond to how she looks rather than what she says here. It stands out. It is not a conscious choice. It is how I respond to her in the moment. I trust my noticing.

H6: 'Know'. Helen takes refuge in thinking. I remain with her facial expression.

R6: Again a choice, but not very consciously made, to reflect back to Helen her facial expression. However, this is based on four sessions of being aware that Helen, ever the computer scientist, is happier thinking about her thoughts than feeling her feelings.

R7. A question. There is a danger of pushing Helen into a corner with this. I know that we relate well enough for her to say that she doesn't want to go there. Strictly speaking, all questions are directive. But I actually *want*—quite passionately—to know about her feelings. There is enough trust between her and me to risk this. At the level of theory, I could well be in touch with bits of GESTALT theory, or with Gendlin's FOCUSING. Both point to experience as being felt *in the body*. But I am not thinking

H10: It just stupid. I'm a grown woman.

R10: When you can't speak, it feels stupid. (Softly, with affection.) *You* feel stupid?

H11: So daft!!! I might have to leave. I can't hack it. I'm frightened I can't hack it!

R11: It frightening … I can't speak out … I can't hack it. I might have to give up all I've worked for.

about that at the time. Whatever I have thought about it in the past, this theory is now simply incorporated into Richard's repertoire of awareness and responses.

R10: Having been a little directive for a moment, tenderness is important. But I do care for Helen. So it's natural. Good grief, this proficient, competent, smart, young woman feels debilitatingly stupid. I think of her as a stuck child in the face of a harsh teacher. It tickles memories of infant school for me, very fleetingly.

*For another four or so minutes, Helen and Richard explore the quality of being frightened and its links to failure.*

R23: And I'm wondering, Helen, if this is how it was with your Dad. Sometimes you just could not speak, when he got so angry.

H24: No, that's not it at all! With Dad, I used to go up to my room and just do whatever I wanted to any way, whatever he said. I liked that. It didn't matter what he was on with. He could shout all he liked. I did my thing. It felt lovely. Pretty defiant.

R24: I guess I feel astonished by that. I had sort of assumed that it was going to be the same.

H25: No, it wasn't. (Pause, then with a firm or even defiant

R23: The structure of the session is that Helen wanted to talk about her parents. It seems to me as if the link between Gerald and her Dad is there for her, but yet to emerge. It's a matter of timing. Links and interpretations belong to the client. My image is that her ACTUALISING TENDENCY is saying: now I'm ready to think about it. That is the whole session perspective. But it is my initiative, my FRAME OF REFERENCE, which makes the link at this point.

H24: And I have allowed myself to be sucked in by the idea of TRANSFERENCE. (Damn it!)

tone.) You can't be right all the time you know. (Laughter.)

R25: Yep! I've been chasing a white rabbit down a burrow, and suddenly it's disappeared on me! (Pause) Something's changed, then. You used to stand up, inside yourself, to Dad's temper, but it's a different thing with Gerald?

H26: Very different. I used to be quite the rebel. (A long pause, and a quizzical but pained look crosses Helen's face.) Then Marcel happened.

R27: Marcel?

H28: He was my MSc supervisor. He was a bugger to all of us. We learned to toe the line with Marcel.

R28: With him, you had to do as you were told!

H29: My rebel gave up.

R29: It's like the pendulum has swung. You used to be a bit of a rebel. You could go off and ignore Dad's outbursts. But now you feel you have to knuckle down.

H30: It swung OK. And it's swung too far. (Helen smiles and looks a little excited.) And I guess what I need to do is to get back to somewhere in the middle.

R25: I like my image of the white rabbit—an echo of *Alice in Wonderland*—because it is important for me to have got it wrong and be OK. This is not just about the counsellor not needing to be an expert. I feel the flicker of joy of having alighted upon a parallel to Helen's life experience. It's OK, even with the bumptious Gerald, to be wrong.

H29: Echoes of configurations of self, here.

R29: I do not know for certain what happened here, within me. I can read this as just an image that is part of an empathic response. However, it will form part of a major challenge to Helen's way of thinking. That will be from my FRAME OF REFERENCE.

H30: The pendulum image produces the smile and the slight excitement in Helen. Why? By now I know her well enough to recognise that she has a strong preference for thinking, and likes to solve prob-

R30: (Using hands to illustrate). The pendulum has swung. You used to be here, the rebel, but now you've swung right over here. (Helen nods.) And you want to get back to the middle.

H31: Yes. That's the answer.

R31: Go on. Say more.

H32: To get back to the middle. (Pause.)

R32: Helen, I guess, well … I see what you are getting at, but I don't see what it means really, to get back to the middle.

H33: Not to give in so much. (Pause.)

R33: I think I'm having problems with this pendulum. (Helen laughs gently.) You see it's a continuum. Two dimensions. (She nods, looks interested.) And I want to think of it more like a triangle.

H34: So how does that work for you?

R34: Well, I don't know what is in the middle of this baseline. Halfway between rebel and compliant Helen. But if I look at the apex, up here, I can begin to imagine you actually finding your voice again—saying what you think. And that feels different to me.

lems. It is, after all, how she makes her living. At times this can take her away from feelings. However, her strongly preferred way of processing, as long as it is kept in touch with what she feels, is a good way for Helen to get change to happen. (And I am certainly about to learn that.)

H32: I treat this with frank suspicion, within me. It's too neat. What does it mean? It is Helen's problem-solving at work. She uses the image of the pendulum to find a solution. But it does not mean much, perhaps. I could have followed Helen's perception, but that would have been INCONGRUENT of me.

R33: This is from deep within my own FRAME OF REFERENCE—and another way of thinking. Had it not connected, then I would have needed to find a way back towards my client. A risk. Yet, the triangle image introduces another possibility; that Helen might experiment with CONGRUENCE.

## Outcome

Clients never cease to amaze me in their flexibility and creativity. Most clients will become more CONGRUENT within therapy, but it is almost always an unconscious process for them. Yet, Helen proved able to take CONGRUENCE as a conscious goal, and to use it. It actually works for her, doing it like that. She is a problem-solver. Given the right emotional support and awareness, she can experiment with Gerald, get back something of the rebel, but this time put it into words rather than just go and hide. Glorious!

## What happened here?

In previous sessions, I had got to know Helen as a person who is able to contact her feelings relatively well, but who has a strong preference for thinking and for problem solving. I have experienced her anxiety and depression, and her sense that it connects with conflict at work. At the beginning of the session, in line with the theory of the ACTUALISING TENDENCY, Helen has reached a point at which her relationship with her parents, and in particular her father, was becoming available to her. A penny was dropping. I listened to Helen from two perspectives. The first was her memory and her recreated experience of fear at her father's anger. The second was Helen's awareness of her presenting problem of conflict at work. Helen holds both aspects in this session. Suddenly she recognises a parallel between them.

At the same time I am also listening for Helen's quite unusual way of processing her experience. She can feel her emotions all too clearly at times, but she sees her thinking abilities as the key to change. She is a problem solver. I invite her to feel her scaredness of Gerald. This feeling is EMBODIED. She can sense it as if it lived in particular place within her. It stops her talking. In terms of theory, I recognise that I am helped to understand Helen's process here both by GESTALT therapy and by the work on EMBODIED meaning done by Carl Rogers' colleague, Eugene Gendlin (1980). I am willing to take the risk of being a little directive here. As I suspect, this does help Helen. If it had not done so, I would have needed to find my way back into her FRAME OF REFERENCE. This can feel awkward. It is very important to know the difference between a suggestion like this, that takes the client on in *her* (and not just my) exploring, and one that interrupts something that matters which is going on already. Any movement into directing the client's process, however briefly, must be respectful of what is already going on (Rennie, 1998, Chapter 7). Theory needs to have depth. It becomes part of our ability to think, to recognise and to respond. Otherwise, it is just a source of tools and bright ideas, which are to be avoided.

My empathic responding to Helen introduces two METAPHORS into the conversation. METAPHORS, and any picture language, are important in that they have a richness and indefiniteness of meaning which can facilitate the client's exploration. Strictly speaking, both METAPHORS are from my own FRAME OF REFERENCE. Yet there is a major difference between them. The first METAPHOR, of the pendulum, is an attempt to express, in a new way, what Helen has said. It is a summary. It is guileless in that I am concerned only to respond to Helen's saying.

The second, however, is a picture which is a response to my not believing Helen's rather artificial solution of a 'return to the middle'. It is therefore directive, an offer of another way of seeing what is needed. Yet it is also an empathic response to Helen's preference for problem-solving. I take my cue from Helen, but offer her a new image to work with in her way.

## CONCLUSION

In this session, I spend most of my time trying to understand Helen and to respond to her empathically. The relationship itself, the whole of who we are together, is non-directive. Yet, there are moments when I feel free to be directive. This is different from CLASSICAL CLIENT-CENTRED THERAPY (Sanders, 2006, Chapter 12).

At no point do I consciously decide to use pre-prepared tools or tricks of the trade. I want always to respond from within me to what the client is saying or doing. While I am aware of at least four pieces of theory from other approaches—TRANSFERENCE; GESTALT thinking on bodily experience; FOCUSING; and configurations of self—each is so integrated that they briefly inform me, but do not become conscious tools. I know what they tell me, but my way of being within me remains fairly constant. Notwithstanding this, I notice that the idea of TRANSFERENCE seduced me into a mistake.

The final METAPHOR is a creative move on my part. Helen likes thinking and looks for solutions. I offer her another way of thinking. The METAPHOR of the triangle offers an alternative to her idea of a midway point between obstinacy and compliance: CONGRUENCE. To my delight, Helen not only seizes upon my observation, but over the following two sessions makes it perfectly clear that she is using it creatively herself.

In this she is unusual. Most clients would not be able to become more CONGRUENT by an act of will. Mercifully, Helen is less acquainted with person-centred theory than I am. So, blissfully unaware, she faces the fear of speaking what she feels, practises a rather fragile calmness to her CONGRUENCE and shows the ability to change her relationship with Gerald, and her consequent level of depression.

That which is IDIOSYNCRATIC in my response to Helen is spontaneous and yet considered. It strives to be in tune with Helen's way of processing her interactions with the world. I simultaneously offer empathy to her keener feelings and explore ways of thinking about how she is.

# 8

# SMALL-SCALE PRACTITIONER RESEARCH

> One of the chief sources of job satisfaction experienced by many counsellors is the sense of continually learning about human nature in response to the lives and personal worlds that the clients allow them to enter. As part of the process, practitioners may find themselves with 'burning questions' ... that can only be answered by doing some research. (McLeod, 1994: 3)

In spite of the hopeful words above, McLeod points out that there is evidence, in particular from the United States, that counsellors 'do not read research articles, and do not consider research to be particularly relevant to their work' (McLeod, 1994: 1).

Research has a difficult image for many counsellors, I suspect. Many will receive one or another popular or learned practice journal with pleasure. Other people's reflections on practice can be felt as an aid to one's own counselling. Yet, far fewer, I suspect, welcome the sound of a research journal dropping onto the front-door mat. Research can feel dry, with difficult to grasp methodologies, best left to academics.

While indeed this stereotype does have some weight to it, counselling research comes in many forms and for many purposes. Published research does have to be formal, and to have a method that is critically chosen and strictly adhered to. Without these qualities, it would not carry the weight of evidence. Evidence-based practice is of increasing importance not least to those who fund therapy. However, other sorts of activity are also research. Research need only be an ordered response to the practitioners' curiosity about, and enjoyment of, their work with clients.

Practitioner research is going on throughout therapy. Whenever I pay attention not just to the client immediately, but to the quality of the whole process of the work, then that is research. What do I want to discover, when I listen to the client? A number of important questions come to my mind that relate to our task of monitoring the quality of the work we do:

1. How does my client experience me?
2. Am I sufficiently consistent in my way of being to be trustworthy for my client?
3. Does my client feel able to contradict me? What is the power dynamic within the relationship? Perceived? Actual? The same or different?
4. Do I understand the client in such a way that she can perceive my empathy and acceptance? (The sixth of Rogers' (1957) SIX CONDITIONS of therapy.)
5. Can I accept who the client is, and in particular her presenting issues?
6. Does the client's material take me to parts of my self that I am ill at ease with?

There can be many other research questions. They resemble topics for exploration in supervision. There is no hard and fast boundary between an 'objective' enquiry about the quality of the therapeutic relationship and the therapist's personal issues that need to be faced. We are engaged in meeting another person. We cannot do this until we can be ourselves, in full and fluent awareness of our limitations. Clients can sense and be terrified by our hollow spaces. (But I will say more of personal development in the next chapter.)

A vision of research that is small-scale, ongoing and personal might in fact turn out to be frightening for another reason. It touches upon our humanity. We might be found out for our darker side. Yet, how can we encounter another person if the darkness within us frightens us. Bob Hobson was, for many years, a trainer, a consultant therapist and a Reader in Psychotherapy at the University of Manchester. He was prone to tell students who asked him what was good preparatory reading for his course that they should start with the Bible and Shakespeare. This was not the answer many wanted! Deeply imbued with the PSYCHODYNAMIC tradition, and yet deeply sceptical of interpretation, he believed with a passion in DIALOGUE. He marked out those therapists who could not engage, because they had not done the personal work, as either opaque or punitive (Hobson, 1985: 200–6). Small-scale research and personal development go hand in hand. Being open and honest about who we are for our clients can feel disturbing at first, but I never fail to sense a thrill whenever I have personal evidence that the client derives something worthwhile from my presence. It is a tougher job to take on board my shortcomings, but they are just as important.

This is true for all therapists, but especially so for those who take an integrative slant on life. When we are committed to hold together all that life might offer, in our meetings with clients, then we access differing parts of ourselves and differing aspects of our knowing at different times. I can think of this in Transactional Analysis terms or not on any occasion, but that is superficial. All half-decent therapists access different aspects of themselves with different clients and at different times (Mearns & Thorne, 2000: 138–40). Therefore the more we are free to practise and the further we are away from the mere portrayal of therapy and the CORE CONDITIONS, the more we are ethically obliged to check how we are.

Below, I suggest a number of ways to explore your own safety and consistency of practice and personal development.

## How do I feel about you?

In 2002, I moved from teaching therapy to working as a counsellor at the University Warwick. (It has been a joyous transition, because high-volume, intense practice is fascinating, stimulating and has finally convinced me that people have a remarkable knack of tapping their resources to reveal healing.) As part of my move, I became aware that I was not comfortable with working with those with eating disorders.

At the same time, I met 'Janet', a young priest who had not only experienced some years of anorexia in adult life, but had then gone on to use this in training churches to incorporate people with eating disorders into their communities. Church communities are both informally and liturgically strongly based around common meals. Who dare not eat?

I made certain that Janet would be willing to work with me on an exploration of my own personal position. We met for one, two-hour session. I wrote down my reflections. Janet reviewed these, offered possible corrections and then approved them for publication as Worsley (2003). I carried into this meeting a strong idea of what encounter was about in terms of Martin Buber's I–Thou, as well as a first intuition that my issue with anorexics is that some underlying fear or discomfort causes me to see them as precisely 'anorexics' rather than 'Thous' (Buber, 1958). It seemed as if, for me, the diagnostic category, anorexic, eclipsed them as whole human beings.

I was struck by Janet's graciousness in helping me see what might be difficult for me. This is crucially important in that what I was doing was saying to her: 'You are the sort of person to whom I cannot offer unconditional positive regard. Can you help me with this?' This could have been painful for Janet. I would never say that to a client, past or present, without sound evidence that she would be safe within the research. It was that Janet had decided to use her experience as a training resource publicly, within the life of the church, that made this interview ethically responsible. Be very careful to check out, in supervision, the ethics of any personal research, however low-key or small-scale, even the odd enquiry at the end of a session.

The learning for me was not so much in a measurable and shareable piece of information or theory. It was in the personal growth that came from the encounter. I knew that I would be different with others presenting with eating disorders. (Such knowledge, of course, is provisional and open to self-deception.) I also learned afresh the power of encounter. Three years and more on, I can work with people who happen to be anorexic with much more comfort and acceptance. I am grateful to Janet.

From time to time, small-scale research is a wise way to tackle issues of personal attitude that might get in the way of the client being heard as a unique individual. However, the more formal and time-consuming they are the less frequently they can take place. The ethics of such encounters is also a matter of great delicacy. There are smaller and less hazardous ways of checking out.

## The follow-up interview

When I worked in medical general practice as a practice counsellor, it was possible to find time to invite back a number of clients for a follow-up interview after three months. The expectation of this interview from the client's point of view was that it was to assess their progress and to give them a chance to explore any remaining issues. Therefore, as a matter of transparency and honesty, that had to be the main focus of the session. However, even within the constraints of that agreement it was possible to ascertain how the therapeutic relationship had gone.

**Illustrative example**: Dave had come to me about relational issues. We had explored his pattern of relationships, past and present. He had been, at first, very hurt by the way women in his life had mistreated him (from his perspective). Gradually, he became aware that, although he was well-intentioned, he gave his partner little quality time. At one point, he arrived and declared that the penny had dropped. I was puzzled as to what he had thought. 'If I can listen to Veronica like you have listened to me, that would be really good, wouldn't it?' I felt a frisson of delight at this, and he went away to experiment with listening. It helped. However, Veronica and he had had sexual problems, particularly after their twin children left home to work away, within five months of each other. At one point, I used the GESTALT cycle of awareness as a way of helping him think about his reactions sexually. He had responded well to this.

On Dave's three-month follow-up, we spent most of the hour thinking about how his relationship now was, and what he had got from therapy in general. In the midst of it, I said that I felt a bit conscious of the diagram we had drawn together. I did not usually work quite like that, I explained. I enquired how he had found it. He said it was useful. Yet, he would say that, wouldn't he? I persisted. Had he felt that I had interrupted the other things we were doing? Had I intruded into his private life too far? Did he feel he had had the chance not to agree to look at that?

I had to be aware of the limited time I had to satisfy my own research need, because the session was essentially for Dave. However, I do note the observation by David Brazier (1993) that part of the healing process is for the client to be able to experience his altruism towards the therapist. In small-scale research situations, I normally find that clients are far happier to give me some time and attention for my needs than I expect them to be. They will often process this in terms of helping others. I do not doubt this conscious motive, but I fancy, as well, that their catering for my need establishes a power balance that goes beyond the normal range of therapy, in which the fundamental pattern is that the client, and not the therapist, is expressing an overt need.

The key quality of the follow-up has to be a shared curiosity about what happened, in which the therapist is genuinely open to the possibility that some parts of therapy were not good, and can say that to the client; that the therapist is non-defensive about this; that she is able to learn from any negatively perceived aspects of the therapy; that she is able to be honest about the client's reaction and her feelings about it; and above all that she is able to permit and welcome whatever it is that the client has to say.

That sounds fine, but there is a problem. This sort of moment-by-moment research relies upon there being a good therapeutic relationship in place. Therefore, it is easier to research successful rather than compromised relationships. Yet it is the mistakes which we make that carry the greatest learning for us.

## In-session research

Some years ago, a supervisee told me that her tutor had said that she should always ask the client for feedback at the end of each session, because that kept the power balance right. This seemed very much to me like a rule, an 'ought', which had some virtue but which at heart should not be trusted. 'What do you think the client feels about this?' I asked. A few moments of thought produced the tentative observation: 'Wouldn't it get in the way at times?' I added that there would be times I would be massively pissed off with it, session after session. It would invade the ending, my taking away where we were. I would wonder why a good therapist would need this endless checking. In any case, if it had been a bad session, dare I say this? Haven't I got to please my therapist just like so many other people in my life? The supervisee took the point. Even straight feedback on how a session has gone is complex. There can be no rules.

However, within any session, the therapist can empathise with the client's experience of the session itself, just in the way she empathises with the content of what the client is saying. Empathy can be for the client's experience of the conversation as well as that of what is being talked of. The tentativeness and tenderness of therapy are so important here (Thorne, 1992: 94) because it is in the ability of the therapist to take risks, without needing to be right, that real relating, DIALOGUE and encounter can take root. Therefore, the therapist is both free and constrained to discover how it is with the client, within the flow of the session itself. The therapist is most free when honesty, trust and transparency are also in full flow. She is most constrained because in that same tender space the needs of the client must transcend her own need to know. To research from within the movement of therapy is a finely judged art.

My only rule of thumb is that, if I feel self-conscious of what I am doing because it does not feel wholly in tune with my usual way of being, I can check it out; but if the client is engaged within herself in process, then anything that I might do could interrupt her. Only research when it seems crucial and when the client is available without interruption to her process.

## CONCLUSION

Research comes under many guises. It is all important, but the small-scale research of the practitioner is particularly significant for its ethical commitment to the quality of the client's experience. There is always the need to balance the freedom to practise with caution, as the thinking through of different elements of therapy in preceding chapters shows. There is a fine judgement to be made between an ethical need to check out how the client is, the need for the client not to be interrupted, and the problem that clients who feel least secure in the relationship will be least able to say this. Yet practitioner research, if taken in a careful but relaxed spirit, is a source of great joy. Some of my most moving encounters have come out of the shared recognition that something went well that was beyond the capacity and control of either of us. This attentiveness to client process is also part of the therapist's commitment to know where she needs to pay attention to her own personal or professional development.

# 9

# INTEGRATING THE SELF: A CONCLUSION

> *Dialogue* entails the recognition of the other person as an experiencing subject. In a simultaneous acting and being acted upon, knowing and being known, there is the mutual creation of a feeling-language: 'I and you' becomes 'I-Thou'. Empathy, a one-way apprehension of what Joe Bloggs is experiencing, moves towards a mutual understanding in which Joe and I are at one and alone together. A hyphen is necessary and I term this relationship *aloneness togetherness*. (Hobson, 1985: 194, original italics)

## Introduction

On the surface, much of this book has been about the way of integrating different insights from other approaches into the person-centred model. I have stressed the need for coherence between the core model and what is to be integrated as well as being careful about how particular insights impact upon practice.

This way of thinking is rooted in PHENOMENOLOGY. The world is not directly perceived. Rather, all that we perceive is mediated to us by our own internal processes. No outsider can correct the image we have of ourselves by protesting that he or she sees very clearly how we are. There is no more painful way of knowing this truth for me than to sit with a person who is terribly thin, with ankles and knees and elbows protruding through parchment-like skin, while that person protests that of course they are terribly fat. No protest touches that person's way of seeing herself.

How we think governs what we see. This does not mean that there is not truth to be seen, but that our seeing of it is subjective. We see the world through our own, preconceived world-view. This is true of life on large and small scales alike. How the therapist thinks will deeply influence what she is able to hear from the client. For instance, counsellors who have not worked upon their emotional awareness of their own death will not be able to hear clients engaging with their mortality.

When we integrate new elements of theory into our counselling model, it is as if we are willing to pick up another lens through which to look. We are willing to risk a new perspective. The looking is always provisional, never certain. In looking we confront, within ourselves, a tendency to believe that our own ways of thinking are uniquely right. This is a narrow and closed view of life, not at all the same thing as adhering to the philosophy and principles of our core model. Integration in this sense would be a necessary and enriching way to think about therapy, even if it amounted to nothing more than thinking about different types of theory.

However, there is more to it than this. Integrating theory is the tip of the iceberg. What really counts is my integration as a person. In this chapter, I can only offer a few intuitions about becoming a more integrated person. It is through integration and maturity that I can hope to enter into DIALOGUE in the way that Bob Hobson talks at the head of this chapter. When we encounter another human being we unwittingly make available the whole of ourselves. Nothing can be held back, and nothing of who we are is irrelevant. This is not about conscious self-disclosure, but about the fact that the partner in encounter can 'see' with infinite depth, even when neither of us is aware of it.

I want to begin thinking about integration and maturity in terms of a recent everyday experience of mine: going for a country walk.

## WALKING, EXPERIENCE AND METAPHOR

Early one summer's morning, I set off in glorious sunlight under vast, blue skies, to walk along the river bank near to where I live. I was, at the time, writing a chapter of this book, on existentialism and therapy. At first, I wandered fairly aimlessly along, simply enjoying the easing of stiffness in my limbs and the depth of breathing fresh air. I glimpsed nosily into others' front windows and admired gardens. After a while my mind felt some refreshment, a clarity that echoed the crisp air of morning. My skin felt the coolness and the growing warmth of the day's return. I was in a sort of light reverie, neither focusing upon what I saw and felt and smelt, nor failing wholly to note my surroundings.

After a while, I decided that it would be useful to use the time productively. I needed to clarify an issue in my own head. I began to play with material from the chapters I had recently read. It was like solving a puzzle. Thoughts came, were inspected and some retained, some dismissed. It felt organised, like work. Yet, imperceptibly my mind returned to its light reverie. Each of the chapters I was thinking about was concerned with mortality. This has inhabited much of my life. As a parish priest I used to take two or three funerals a week. I believe that coming to terms with my dying is important. At the moment a close friend is facing her own, imminent death. Grace and anger interweave.

For a few moments, but I know not how long, it was as if the thoughts of death blocked out everything from my sight. Then, suddenly, the sight of a willow tree, vivid lime green in early summer, arrested my thoughts and my walking. I stared. Death is no *idea*. Whatever else, it is my absence from this scene, and the death of vivid lime green from me. The reverie was overturned. I gulped in the immediacy of my senses. I clung hard to the present. Only afterwards could I image the meaning of this for me.

I would hate to call this a mystical experience if, by that, it sounds either special or pretentious. The most important element of this was its ordinariness. Yet, I note how I moved between radically different parts of myself. I was in a vague dream-state, close to the waking surface of life. I was looking and seeing, but with idle curiosity. A conscious decision had me 'work' at the thought of death. This felt productive. I had to concentrate. Yet the motion of walking and the piercing purity of light threw me unintentionally back to a deeper and intrinsically personal contact with my own dying, and my friend's. I had the curious sensation of having thoughts and yet not being 'close' to these thoughts. The question of existence had me moving into the unconscious dynamic of the existential moment.

The absence of intense contact with the present, a timeless

reverie, suddenly broke under the force of the lime-greenness of newly grown leaves. Thrown back into the present, I saw—saw, but not yet felt, sight without emotion—the concreteness of demise. I clung onto my senses. Only afterwards, a few yards down the path and past the fishermen who greeted me, did I recognise any meaning.

I am now aware that in a few instants of time I was in touch with a number of modes of my being. There was everyday depth in this. Mortality and leaves interwove. Each movement of the miniature drama stood for an aspect of myself, a process which is me being alive. I could not distinguish its literal from its METAPHORICAL meaning. The generation of meaning penetrated the whole event, and yet at its most REFLEXIVE had to await the time for me to integrate and process it. Had I not thought about it, had I not written about it, there would have been loss.

The greenness of the tree, for instance, was both a vivid, physical experience, a GESTALT completed in an instant. It is also a continuing METAPHOR. It points beyond itself. There is nothing in particular that the tree is *like*. The tree stands for a complex of feelings and hoping and loving. There is a SURPLUS OF MEANING in it, its existential disclosure of my capacity to be alive.

The next three sections of this chapter are brief reflections upon Propositions XVII–XIX of Rogers' (1951) NINETEEN PROPOSITIONS. The aim is to understand more of how our own and the client's experiencing can move towards integration. Integration is a move towards being a system that is increasingly fluent.

## FLUENCY AND AWARENESS

> XVII) *Under certain conditions, involving primarily complete absence of any threat to the self-structure, experiences which are inconsistent with it may be perceived, and examined, and the structure of self revised to assimilate and include such experiences.* (Rogers, 1951: 517)

I suggest that while this, and the next two propositions, are, in their original context, about the client, they apply equally to the therapist. That is to say, it is the therapist's way of being which is healing, in the way that Bob Hobson claims at the head of this chapter. Rogers argues in this proposition that healthy being is about the ability to admit to awareness those experiences which require us to modify our SELF-STRUCTURE. This is not just a once-and-for-all correction of some major distortion, but can be an on-going process implemented on a small scale. In meeting another person at existential depth, I will display this quality. The other person will impact upon me. Therefore the deeper the meeting the more I will be called upon to modify my SELF-STRUCTURE to meet the otherness of the other person. People change us radically when we can bear to let them close to us.

This may seem a rather exotic point, but is also part of my everyday experience. When I meet someone, I tend to put them, at first sight, into familiar and comfortable categories. Depth of meeting breaks open my categories, and thus my view of myself and of the world I create and inhabit.

What the terms 'real' and 'genuine' signify in a relationship, besides their more usual denotations, is being fluent in awareness of oneself and others. It is not being perfect, whatever that would mean. Rogers never suggests that to be FULLY FUNCTIONING is to have arrived. That is not a helpful METAPHOR. Rather it is to be in a sufficiently fluent process. The client needs to experience in the therapist a flow of experience which both accurately maps to the outside world and is also 'at home' within the therapist.

Being real, being fluent in awareness, is at times a battle. It requires that I look at what I really feel about the client's attitude towards me, whether or not that has angered me or hurt me. I then need to decide how to express this so that it is therapeutically helpful for the client. Some therapists can be present in this vulnerable way. Others keep a veneer of calm even in stormy waters. The client will sense that it is a veneer, a defence. Indeed, they may recognise at some level that it is a defence they know well enough from the inside. 'And so being angry or being attacked really is frightening. Even my therapist shuts up shop when this happens.' It is one of the disagreements I would have with those who believe that the therapist is a psychodynamic BLANK SCREEN, but I have also seen this played out by at least one person-centred therapist in a major fashion.

I need to integrate into my being with clients my ability to feel my anger and my fear, and also my love. In supervision, the most important question on so many occasions is: How can you get that into the room in a useful way? In a final session with a client, we were reviewing how the journey had been, mainly for him but also for me. I said that I had experienced him in the later sessions as so much easier to be with. He looked at me with a not very typical twinkle in his eye and said: 'Blimey! Was I really that awkward for you?' 'Indeed you were!' I replied. At that point something shifted for him, I do not know quite what. Yet, I think he felt a relief that the rigidity that inhabited him, unspoken of by anyone, was not only easing up, but could actually be mentioned.

## Encounter

> XVIII) *When the individual perceives and accepts into one consistent and integrated system all his sensory and visceral experiences, then he is necessarily more understanding of others and is more accepting of separate individuals.* (Rogers, 1951: 520)

On the surface, Rogers here claims that when the client's level of CONGRUENCE increases, that person can accept others as themselves and, therefore, as different. By extension it is also true that the therapist's unconditional positive regard is increased as her CONGRUENCE grows. In other words, integration of all parts of the self by the therapist into 'one consistent and integrated system' is a prerequisite of encounter. But why?

Rogers' thinking, as expressed in Proposition XVIII, is that the unintegrated elements of the personality are repressed and result in a dissonance between the SELF-STRUCTURE and the process of ORGANISMIC VALUATION. As we have seen above (Chapter 3), Mearns and Thorne's (2000) thinking about CONFIGURATIONS OF SELF changes the way we see this. In fact, the repressed material can, together with other material, form complex patterns or subpersonalities, which are, in different degrees, either cut off from each other or in fruitful communication with each other, or which give birth to new configurations which are healthier. The new situation involves internal dialogue and minimises internal splits within the personality. In the case of Dave Mearns' (1994) example of Elizabeth, the repressed material is at first lodged with two CONFIGURATIONS. The 'nun' represents the INTROJECTED CONDITIONS OF WORTH seen as having positive life value: 'If I do as I am told, I will be accepted'. The 'little girl' represents the organismic but disorganised rejection of the 'nun'. The process of therapy can be seen as:

1. a growing awareness of the two CONFIGURATIONS. They are named and as such come into existence in a new way.
2. a growing dialogue between the two configurations.
3. the creation of a third CONFIGURATION which does not split off material, but integrates the whole of experience into a life-stance that is tolerant of pain and ambivalence.

However, I suggest that there is more happening within the therapeutic relationship than this.

I have, from time to time, seen therapists at work in the training situation where there are large and difficult INCONGRUENCES at play. I notice that some—but not all—clients experience this, even when it is not clearly present in the room, as a lurking, irrational threat. It seems likely that the integration of the therapist is experienced consciously, or otherwise, by the client as a resource, as part of the process of healing.

In order to maintain a free and open DIALOGUE, a DIALOGUE that can take risks as well as be containing, the therapist has to be able to maintain open DIALOGUE within herself, to a sufficient degree. There is a parallel process between the interpersonal DIALOGUE of client-with-therapist and the intrapersonal dialogue of therapist-with-her-selves. It is therefore not surprising that there is a parallel process between the healthy internal DIALOGUE of any therapist and her ability to have an open dialogue with other schools of therapy. Both concern the acceptance of the different as creative rather than the need to split off the different as 'heretical' (Thorne, 1992: 94).

## EXISTENCE AND SIGNS

> XIX) *As the individual perceives and accepts into his self-structure more of his organic experiences, he finds that he is replacing his present value* system—*based so largely upon* INTROJECTIONS *which have been distortedly symbolised—with a continuing organismic valuing* process. (Rogers, 1951: 522, original emphases)

In Proposition XIX, Carl Rogers signals the movement from systems of 'oughts' to the ORGANISMIC VALUING PROCESS. There is one ludicrous misreading of Rogers that simply condemns him as an amoral, 1960s, West-Coast liberal, an intellectual hippy. Nothing could be further from the truth. His dialogues with both Buber and especially Tillich show him to be a person who is deeply committed to a moral view of life (Kirschenbaum & Henderson, 1990a, 1990b). Rogers' point is that we cannot take refuge in preformed and rigid codes. This does not mean that we cannot subscribe to communal codes, but we have to work towards a personal and critical ownership: we must be in process of continually facing and integrating our very own decisions about life's demands into our way of being.

I am continually amused by clients who say: 'You shouldn't upset other people, should you?' I know that my amusement is based in part on my own defences. I lived with this one for too long. I will normally respond: 'Why not?' The point is that the client is at, one level, right. The person who makes a living by upsetting others is often stuck in a difficult and unhealthy pattern. However, the client usually means: to upset anyone at all is absolutely unthinkable! This stance leaves the client open to moral blackmail as well as the paradox that often one has to upset Joe in order not to upset Freda. Life is messy. There is, in any case, something wrong with the notion of navigating only by upset. The client can often be fooled by the apparent common-sense element of not (deliberately and gratuitously) upsetting someone, into holding a very rigid 'principle' that it is 'wicked' to upset anyone, ever. We need to evaluate all situations as both complex and immediate.

It is, I hope, obvious that a therapist needs to have worked through her own CONDITIONS OF WORTH. There must be a fluent, internal DIALOGUE. However, the ability to evaluate organismically, to be engaged in an active quest for awareness, has far-reaching consequences for therapy. When the therapist becomes accustomed to the in-depth nature of organismic evaluation, then the way truth is listened for in therapy shifts. Metaphor becomes a key.

METAPHORS, particularly in counselling, have an interesting quality (Ricoeur, 1975/1986). When a client explores a METAPHOR, the meaning of it never runs out; there is always something more that can be said. This is often called the metaphor's SURPLUS OF MEANING. When clients explore METAPHORS, any form of picture language, anything which can have a SURPLUS OF MEANING, then the therapist must be free enough within herself to search with the client for new meaning, and be prepared for that meaning to impact upon her as well as the client. We need to be open to new meanings in our life, and that can be frightening. When we flee for cover, for false certainties—and all certainties, barring a few rather boring ones, are likely to be false—then we cease to be able to hear and accompany the client, who is often at one of the most productive stages of therapy.

However, METAPHOR is important in thinking about counselling theory. Therapeutic theory is also METAPHORICAL. This might seem odd at first, but experiment with it. Think about the configuration of the 'nun' in Mearns' (1994) case of Elizabeth. The nun is of course not a real nun. That is not, though, what I mean. Rather, the fact that the CONFIGURATION functions in a cut-off way from the rest of Elizabeth at first, and that it shifts and changes, shows that all that we perceive of mental process is an image, a METAPHOR, for the invisible, underlying brain processes. Thus, if the nun were to disappear we might say that this was important, even healing, but we would not ask where she had gone to!

If most psychological constructs have this METAPHORICAL quality, then this is certainly true of the constructs that make up the different approaches to therapy. My point, then, is that there is a connection between a therapist's openness to meaning and METAPHOR within therapy sessions and her openness to new meaning from others' ways of theorising. Good theory is ambiguous. Therapists must live with this.

Clients who grow seem to me also to be able to live with ambiguity.

## Migrants

For many of my clients who have most inspired affection in me, there has been a journey towards a courageous integration of the testing and the painful parts of themselves into their living. Some MEDICAL MODEL versions of therapy view depression, for instance, as like a bout of 'flu. If we take the drugs, we will get over it. There is much wrong with this view of therapy (Sanders, 2005), not least that those who experience depression find it a far richer experience than a mere illness. Depression, worked through, can be an aspect of maturity, of the ability to see, hold and live with life's ambiguities.

I value poetry for its ability to express the proximity of hope to despair. If we integrate all of who we are into our therapy, we can then develop the right to accompany those who are wise on their journey to wholeness. I offer the words of the Welsh poet, RS Thomas, as a fine example of living on the cusp of hope and despair:

**Migrants**[1]

He is the great void
We must enter, calling
To one another on the way
In the direction from which
he blows. What matter
if we should never arrive
to breed or to winter
in the climate of our conception?

---

1. I am grateful to Bloodaxe Books for their permission to print this poem. 'Migrants' appeared in RS Thomas (1992) *Mass for Hard Times*. Newcastle-upon-Tyne: Bloodaxe.

Enough we have been given wings
And a needle in the mind
To respond to his bleak north.
There are times even at the Pole
When he, too, pauses in his withdrawal,
So that it is light there all night long.

RS Thomas (1992: 80)

Our clients who integrate the bleak creatively into their living become migrants, those who renounce a home in the city of false certainty to inhabit instead their own emotional reality. Integration is, at heart, the incorporation into ourselves of dark and light, so that we may move between the two without fear, reconciled yet hopeful.

## The narrow ridge

> I have occasionally described my standpoint to my friends as the 'narrow ridge'. I wanted this to express that I did not rest on the broad upland of a belief system that includes a series of sure statements about the absolute, but on a narrow, rocky ridge between the gulfs where there is no sureness of expressible knowledge but the certainty of meeting what remains undisclosed. (Buber, 1947: 184)

RS Thomas' *Migrants* expresses the journey of personal integration where darkness and light are alike, and upon which we accompany our clients. This sense of being a person whose wholeness is incarnated in her journeying towards a fluency of living and a peace in dying is one to be shared by therapist and client, as best we may. Yet, at the end of this brief introduction to integrative therapy, we come back full circle to an integration of theory. The words of Martin Buber, above, use the image of the 'narrow ridge' powerfully. We are to inhabit that lofty place, vertiginous, in which we have renounced all false certainty of ideas in order to attain the place of meeting in which the other is yet to be disclosed. We must not cling to false truth, which is truth held too firmly. It would be a bitter irony if those who aspire to such ENCOUNTER cannot free themselves to stand upon the narrow ridge of theory, in which they willingly open themselves to the challenge and insight of other therapists and other schools. There would lurk hypocrisy.

# APPENDIX

# RESOURCES FOR LEARNING

## ORGANISATIONS

World Association for Person-Centered and EXPERIENTIAL Psychotherapy and Counseling (WAPCEPC)
<www.pce-world.org>
British Association for the Person-Centred Approach (BAPCA)
<www.bapca.org.uk>
Association for the Development of the Person-Centered Approach
<www.adpca.org/>

## JOURNALS

*Person-Centered and Experiential Psychotherapies*. The quarterly journal of WAPCEPC (also sent to all BAPCA members as part of their subscription).
*Person-Centered Journal*. The annual journal of the Association for the Development of the Person-Centered Approach.

## WEBSITES

In addition to the organisation websites above, there are some websites which are good 'portals' because they have many links to websites with substantial content regarding person-centred therapy. Since websites occasionally change their URL or simply disappear, I suggest you use this link which has details of over 60 useful sites for counsellors and psychologists, 18 of them person-centred, and the list is added to regularly: <www.pccs-books.co.uk/page.php?xPage=links.html>

## FURTHER READING

Readers will realise that there are hundreds of books and articles which may, or may not, be of interest to you (take a look at the references section of this book!), depending on your level of study and aspirations. If you feel overwhelmed by the sheer number of books available and you want some guidance, these are the books that *I* think are particularly useful and/or important. I have chosen books that are mainly up-to-date, in print and available. This is *not* a definitive list, especially since by the time you are reading this book, a few more will have appeared on the scene.

**To accompany or follow immediately after an 'intermediate' (certificate) course in person-centred therapy**

Merry, T (1995/2006) *Invitation to Person-Centred Psychology*. London: Whurr. Republished (2006) Ross-on-Wye: PCCS Books.

Merry, T (2002) *Learning and Being in Person-Centred Counselling*. Ross-on-Wye: PCCS Books.

Sanders, P (ed) (2004) *The Tribes of the Person-Centred Nation: An introduction to the schools of therapy associated with the person-centred approach*. Ross-on-Wye: PCCS Books.

Tolan, J (2003) *Skills in Person-Centred Counselling and Psychotherapy*. London: Sage.

Tudor, K & Merry, T (2002/2006) *Dictionary of Person-Centred Psychology*. London: Whurr. Republished (2006) Ross-on-Wye: PCCS Books.

**For 'professional' (degree, diploma or Masters) courses in person-centred therapy**

Embleton Tudor, L, Keemar, K, Tudor, K, Valentine, J & Worrall, M (2004) *The Person-Centred Approach: A contemporary introduction*. Basingstoke: Palgrave.

Joseph, S & Worsley, R (eds) (2005) *Person-Centred Psychopathology: A positive psychology of mental health*. Ross-on-Wye: PCCS Books.

Mearns, D (2003) *Developing Person-Centred Counselling*. London: Sage.

Mearns, D & Cooper, M (2005) *Working at Relational Depth in Counselling and Psychotherapy*. London: Sage.

Mearns, D & Thorne, B (2000) *Person-Centred Therapy Today*. London: Sage.

Wyatt, G (Series Editor) (2001/2) *Rogers' Therapeutic Conditions. Volumes 1, 2, 3 & 4*. Ross-on-Wye: PCCS Books. (See references section under Wyatt, 2001; Haugh & Merry, 2001; Bozarth & Wilkins, 2001 and Wyatt & Sanders, 2002.)

Wilkins, P (2003) *Person-Centred Therapy in Focus*. London: Sage.

Worsley, R (2002) *Process Work in Person-Centred Therapy: Phenomenological and existential perspectives*. Basingstoke: Palgrave.

**For professional study in integrative or other approaches**

***Person-centred theory***

Mearns, D (2003) *Developing Person-Centred Counselling*. London: Sage.

Merry, T (2002) *Learning and Being in Person-Centred Counselling*. Ross-on-Wye: PCCS Books.

Sanders, P (ed) (2004) *The Tribes of the Person-Centred Nation: An introduction to the schools of therapy associated with the person-centred approach*. Ross-on-Wye: PCCS Books.

Tudor, K & Worrall, M (2006) *Person-Centred Therapy: A clinical philosophy*. London: Routledge.

Wyatt, G (Series Editor) (2001/2) *Rogers' Therapeutic Conditions. Volumes 1, 2, 3 & 4*. Ross-on-Wye: PCCS Books. (See references section under Wyatt, 2001; Haugh & Merry, 2001; Bozarth & Wilkins, 2001 and Wyatt & Sanders, 2002.)

Worsley, R (2002) *Process Work in Person-Centred Therapy: Phenomenological and existential perspectives*. Basingstoke: Palgrave.

***Existentialism***

Buber, M (1958) *I and Thou*. Edinburgh: T and T Clark.

Cooper, D (1990) *Existentialism*. Oxford: Blackwell.

Macquarrie, J (1972/1991) *Existentialism*. Harmondsworth: Penguin/ Pelican.

Tillich, P (1952/1980) *The Courage to Be*. New Haven: Yale University Press.

***Existential Therapy***

Cohn, HW (1997) *Existential Thought and Therapeutic Practice: An introduction to existential psychotherapy*. London: Sage.

Cooper, M (2003) *Existential Therapies*. London: Sage.

Frankl, V (2004) *Man's Search for Meaning*. London: Rider & Co.

Yalom, ID (2001) *The Gift of Therapy: Reflections on being a therapist*. London: Piatkus.

***Other humanistic theories***

Berne, E (1964/1968) *Games People Play: The psychology of human relationships*. Harmondsworth: Penguin.

Harris, TA (1970/1973) *I'm OK—You're OK*. London: Pan.

Sills, C, Fish, S & Lapworth, P (1995) *Gestalt Counselling*. Bicester: Winslow Press.

Stewart, I & Joines, V (1987) *T.A.Today: A new introduction to transactional analysis*. Nottingham: Lifespace.

Stevens, JO (1971/1989) *Awareness: Exploring, experimenting, experiencing*. Enfield: Eden Grove.

Zinker, J (1978) *Creative Process in Gestalt Therapy*. New York: Random House.

# GLOSSARY

**ACTUALISING TENDENCY** The ability of human beings to seek to fulfil their potential for growth. It has more recently come to be seen that some of what we actualise is not our maximum potential.

**ANGST** Most EXISTENTIAL philosophers and therapists observe that life carries with it a form of anxiety that comes from the very fact of being aware and alive. Called ANGST to differentiate it from pathological anxiety.

**BEHAVIOURISM** A strand of psychology founded in the 1920s by J Watson, the only concern of which is the inputs or stimuli from the outside world and the allegedly resulting behaviour. The internal conditions of the subject are bracketed out. As a *method* it has some uses. It becomes particularly unhelpful when the bracketing out of internal awareness comes to be taken as a dogma about the nature, or even absence, of the reality of human subjective awareness.

**BLANK SCREEN** Orthodox Freudians and some other psychodynamic practitioners see the role of the therapist as avoiding undue human interaction so that they constitute a blank screen upon which clients can project through the process of TRANSFERENCE their significant past and present relationships, which can then be interpreted.

**CLASSICAL CLIENT-CENTRED THERAPY** That version of person-centred therapy which strives to remain close to the core principles as enunciated by Carl Rogers (see Merry, 2004).

**COGNITIVE-BEHAVIOURAL** A form of therapy based on a directive approach to changing patterns of thinking and patterns of behaviour. Mainly about symptom relief. Good practitioners of this approach recognise this, and need to work in other ways with the majority of clients. The danger of not recognising this is that symptoms are suppressed without further structural change. They return in other forms.

**CONDITIONS OF WORTH** Messages from emotionally important people in life, which typically suggest that we have worth *only if* we fulfil a particular condition. We then INTROJECT or internalise this conditionality. It creates an internal tension, INCONGRUENCE, between our SELF-CONCEPT and our ORGANISMIC VALUING of our experience.

**CONFIGURATIONS OF SELF** A pattern of thoughts, feelings and behaviours which form a discrete structure within the personality. This can be based predominantly upon INTROJECTS, but is not necessarily so.

**CONGRUENCE** A sufficient correspondence between the SELF-CONCEPT or

SELF-STRUCTURE of an individual, and the outcome of the organismic evaluation of their experience. When people are CONGRUENT there is little need to repress experience, since it can be realistically accommodated by the SELF-STRUCTURE.

**CONSCIOUSNESS** A major area of study in neuroscience and philosophy as well as psychology. The word points to a number of different phenomena. The most obvious is the fact that humans are aware of their internal and external worlds and the here and now. Also includes the higher capacity to be aware of ,and then to conceptualise, this awareness. D Rennie (2006) refers to this as radical REFLEXIVITY. French philosopher, René Descartes, had seen consciousness as a single and non-material point of eternal awareness and has been very influential in modern culture. However, consciousness is now to be seen as a quality which is very difficult to define, and in which processes that are undoubtedly mental and unconscious can enter into the arena of consciousness. One example of this is in the configured nature of the self described in Chapter 3, above. Person-centred theory has been cautious of the terminology of conscious/unconscious because it echoes with Freudian thinking.

**CONTACT** Otherwise, psychological contact. It is the first of the SIX CONDITIONS OF THERAPY according to Rogers (1957). Contact exists when two people are each capable of impinging upon the other's field of awareness. Some serious forms of mental distress, often referred to as the psychoses, are characterised by a loss of contact. This is an important idea in person-centred PRE-THERAPY, as well as in object relations theory.

**CORE CONDITIONS** Empathy, CONGRUENCE and unconditional positive regard—the qualities of a relationship which act as a summary of the six conditions necessary and sufficient for therapeutic change (Rogers, 1957). While the SIX CONDITIONS are specific to the *therapeutic* relationship, the CORE CONDITIONS can be applied to any relationship.

**DIALOGIC/DIALOGICAL (THERAPY)** Not so much a 'school' as the idea that therapy is DIALOGUE, is relational. It is a deep acknowledgement of the potential made possible by the separateness of client and counsellor in every moment of meeting. Sometimes called 'encounter-oriented approach'. Similar to 'encounter': a meeting at relational depth in which characteristically each participant recognises the otherness of the other. It best symbolised as face to face rather than alongside (Schmid, 1998).

**DIALOGUE** A quality of a relationship that involves meeting at depth, so that each party can engage with the other as a whole human being rather than as an object. This corresponds closely to Martin Buber's (1958) concept of the I–Thou relationship.

**DYSFUNCTION** A distortion in the structure of the personality. In Carl Rogers' terms, it springs usually from the INCONGRUENCE between organismic experiencing and the SELF-CONCEPT.

**ECLECTICISM** The therapeutic practice of selecting a set of procedures from a number of models of therapy. The procedures are thought to correspond to the specific, diagnosed needs of the client.

**EGO STATE** In Transactional Analysis, the condition of being either in Parent, Adult or Child. Each ego state is a phenomenological but, at the same time, stereotypical set of behaviours, thoughts and feelings, which corresponds to a general pattern or role, but the precise details of which are unique to each individual.

**EXISTENTIAL(IST)** Relating to the philosophy of existence. There is a very wide variety of thought within this philosophical tradition, some of it contradicting other parts. Its key themes are the stress upon the subjective, and the consequent task of living one's life under one's own responsibility.

**EXPERIENTIAL** Within the family of person-centred and experiential psychotherapies, the word EXPERIENTIAL marks out those approaches which stress firstly the therapist's concern with the client's process and, for some therapists, a consequent commitment to be directive so as to clarify experience.

**FIGURE AND GROUND** In GESTALT theory, the fact that our experience 'stands out' for us just as a figure stands out on a (back)ground has implications for emotional well-being. Figures have to be closed off, finished, completed in order to resolve tension. Humans have a natural need to complete figures—the Zeigarnick effect—so that a new figure can be embarked upon.

**FOCUSING (-ORIENTED COUNSELLING)** An approach developed by Eugene Gendlin, one of Carl Rogers' students and colleagues, and based on the inner flow of experience. See Campbell Purton, in Sanders, 2004.

**FRAGILE PROCESS** Term coined by Margaret Warner (2000) to indicate a style of being which, amongst many other features (understood by many to be analagous to 'borderline personality disorder'), is very difficult to work with in therapy.

**FRAME OF REFERENCE** The measure by which we make meaning out of reality. The world-view or the surrounding presuppositions about life through which sense is made of any experience. A useful simile might be the relationship between the axes of a graph and its curve. The meaning or the curve can only be seen when it is read against the scale, the frame of reference.

**FULLY FUNCTIONING** In Carl Rogers' thought, the healthy person is able to integrate in-coming experience into the SELF-STRUCTURE without need to repress or deny that experience. It is better seen as fluent process than a sort of psychological nirvana.

**GAME** In Transactional Analysis, any activity that has an ulterior motivation, in which the apparent pay-off and the psychological pay-off are not congruent.

**GESTALT** A German word meaning 'whole'. In psychology, the Gestaltists were those who noted that humans perceive, not individual items, but patterns or whole. For example, when we get home we recognise our own house from its pattern, yet we do not know how many bricks make up the front elevation. GESTALT therapy uses this fact to explore DYSFUNCTION as incomplete gestalts.

**GOOD LIFE, THE** The EXISTENTIAL quality of being fully functioning. Undue moral connotation is a misreading of this term.

**HOLISM** The principle that as humans, as organisms, we have to think of ourselves as a whole, in our entirety, so as to do justice to all aspects of our selves. The opposite is reductionism (analysis by constituent parts, but also a tendency to treat the self as a machine).

**HORIZONTALISATION** One of the key principles of phenomenological reduction (Spinelli, 1989) and hence of all humanistic therapies. Each statement of the client must be given equal weight in the first instance. The complexity of communication guarantees that this is a counsel of perfection.

**HUMANISTIC THERAPIES** A group of therapeutic schools which include person-centred therapy, GESTALT therapy and Transactional Analysis. They have in common a reliance upon the centrality of the whole human being, and particularly as subject of experience, and therefore of PHENOMENOLOGY and its methodologies. EXISTENTIAL therapies have much in common, but are usually not seen as humanistic. In philosophy, American existentialism is often described as humanistic, while its European counterpart is seen as having too bleak a view of humanity to qualify for this accolade.

**IDIOSYNCRATIC** This term was first used by Jerold Bozarth in the mid 1980s. He uses it to signal his desire to remain committed to experiencing the client's FRAME OF REFERENCE, and thus to using the language, and above all the social code and special terms of reference of the client. He sees idiosyncrasy as more about conveying unconditional positive regard than about checking constantly that he has understood the client. He is less committed to the latter than those he sees as purists. (Bozarth, personal correspondence, June 2006.) I use this word therefore in a far broader sense than does Bozarth, but I believe in the same spirit. The IDIOSYNCRATIC is *my own* particular response to the client, sometimes, as with Bozarth, using the client's particular language code, but also, going beyond Bozarth, being open to expressing my responses in my own particular language codes. (See for example Chapter 4, on using the ego-state construct.)

**INCONGRUENCE** See above, CONGRUENCE.

**INTEGRATIVE AND ECLECTIC THERAPIES** A broad group of therapies that take material from more than one school. Integration involves an attempt to create a philosophically and psychologically coherent model for two or more other models or part-models. A good integrative model has the same quality of coherence as a single model. By contrast, ECLECTIC models have a tool-like pick-and-mix quality to them. At best, they believe that specific DYSFUNCTIONS need to be diagnosed and then treated with specific interventions. At worst, they are just plain irresponsible.

**INTERVENTION** Strictly speaking it means 'interference' (to stop something: to intervene). Often used to mean counsellor-response. Not frequently used in person-centred circles, some practitioners preferring to use 'contribution'.

**INTROJECTION/INTROJECTS** The internalisation of material that is simultaneously ignored and acted upon (incorporating it into one's psychological structure without modification and then believing, to some degree, it originated from inside). See INCONGRUENCE. Fritz Perls likens it graphically to taking a bite of apple and swallowing it whole.

**LOCUS OF EVALUATION** The 'place' where the client evaluates incoming experiences. If internal, it is CONGRUENT with the ORGANISMIC VALUING PROCESS. If external, it is often attributable to CONDITIONS OF WORTH.

**MEDICAL MODEL** The use of physical causality and of a diagnosis–treatment model to address in particular mental health issues. The model is based on similarity of symptoms and tends to exclude the personal, subjective element, the mental-mental and mental-physical causal trains, not to mention the social genesis of mental distress. It is not to be confused with scientific thinking about mental health

**METAPHOR** A figure of speech in which an imaginative comparison is made between two elements, so that one is said to *be* the other, rather than said to be *like* the other. For instance: 'You are the centre of the universe'.

**METAPHORICAL (THEORY AS)** It is tempting to see theory as a naïvely realistic statement of mental and psychological processes. Since mental processes are uniquely also brain processes, then theory might better be seen as useful pictures of what is happening, but always an approximation to the actual.

**NECESSARY AND SUFFICIENT CONDITIONS OF THERAPY** are the SIX CONDITIONS set out in Rogers' (1957) paper. These conditions are 'necessary' in that significant psychological change cannot happen without them. They are 'sufficient' in that such change will always happen when they are present.

**NINETEEN PROPOSITIONS** One of Rogers' earlier attempts to summarise his theory of therapy, with a particular stress upon the principles which underpin the theory (Rogers, 1951).

**NON-DIRECTIVE (THERAPY)** is any therapy which seeks to accord freedom to the client to determine the direction, content and process of therapy. There is disagreement in the person-centred world as to whether such a therapy must strive to be non-directive on each and every occasion, or whether non-directivity is a quality of the whole relationship. The second view would permit some 'local' directive interventions and responses.

**ORGANIC CONDITION/DISEASE** A condition or illness with a physical/biological cause (rather than psychological), e.g. brain tumours are physical (organic) entities but symptoms can, in some circumstances, look like the symptoms of psychological distress (mood swings). Also, e.g. delirium (hallucinations and delusions) caused by fever.

**ORGANISMIC VALUING PROCESS** The ability of the human organism—body and mind together—to judge the worth of input from the surrounding world and, therefore, of the self. It is undermined by the oppressive nature of CONDITIONS OF WORTH, which are INTROJECTED and so generate a SELF-CONCEPT which is incongruent with the said ORGANISMIC VALUING PROCESS.

**PHENOMENOLOGY/PHENOMENOLOGICAL** Phenomenology is the philosophical study of what appears to us as we perceive. One of its main lessons is that we do not see 'reality' but construct a version of it. This is an inevitable part of perceiving. It is therefore the basis for not interpreting but persisting in focusing upon the course of the client's experience, in therapy.

**PLATONIC THOUGHT** The thinking of the ancient Greek philosopher, Plato. He believed in the human soul as a single point of immaterial consciousness. This is then detached from physical life. It is the basic stance of the work of the French enlightenment philosopher, René Descartes, and has haunted modern thinking too.

**PRE-THERAPY** This has been developed in the United States by Garry Prouty, and in Europe by others, not least Dion Van Werde and Marlis Pörtner. (Prouty *et al.,* 2002) It is based on the fact that when clients are so cut off that they are PSYCHOTIC, then the task to be undertaken before person-centred therapy is to commence is to re-establish contact (The first of Rogers SIX NECESSARY AND SUFFICIENT CONDITIONS). Pre-therapy involves making very literal and concrete reflections so that the client can begin to experience contact with her own environment.

**PRIMARY PREVENTION RESEARCH** Looking at the factors which predispose people to certain conditions/distress, such as social and environmental conditions, and personal characteristics and experiences.

**PROCESS DIRECTION** In EXPERIENTIAL psychotherapy in particular, the activity of the therapist in instructing the client to experiment with how they process their material.

**PROTOCOL** A set of instructions as in a handbook for how to implement a strategy in therapy. It is increasingly 'popular' with mechanistic therapies, because training then becomes a cheaper matter! This should be regarded by all person-centred practitioners as the spawn of Satan.

**PSYCHODYNAMIC APPROACH** A wide ranging, major approach to therapy, founded on the work of Sigmund Freud. The psychodynamic approach seeks to uncover the unconscious motivations of the client by a process of interpretation.

**PSYCHOTIC** A MEDICAL MODEL classification of range of severe levels of distress in which the person loses the ability to make basic contact (Rogers, 1957, Condition One) with others. There is then a consequent apparent loss of a sense of reality. However, Garry Prouty and others before him have pointed out that contact can be re-established, and that, contrary to appearances, relationship in psychotic people is therefore crucial (Prouty et al., 2002).

**REFLECTIVE PRACTICE** The ethical commitment to practice therapy by a process of reflecting upon the theory of therapy and its links to our self-awareness. It is one of the bases of accountable practice.

**REFLEXIVE (REFLEXIVITY)/REFLEXIVITY AND SPONTANEITY** Because there is no clear-cut line between conscious and unconscious processing, humans exist on a continuum between the spontaneous, which is not thought through, and the reflexive, which is the result of conscious contemplation. While Rogers saw the need to move towards the spontaneous as part of becoming more congruent, a contextually sound balance between the two is needed.

**REPRESSION** The unconscious refusal to admit to full awareness a piece of experience which is unacceptable to the client's SELF-STRUCTURE.

**SELF-CONCEPT** Literally, the way we think about who we are. However, it hovers between conscious and unconscious processing. In Rogers (1951) he uses the phrase SELF-STRUCTURE.

**SELF-STRUCTURE** See above, SELF-CONCEPT.

**SIX CONDITIONS OF THERAPY** In 1957, Carl Rogers set out the six conditions of therapy which he took to be both necessary and sufficient for the implementation of significant psychological change. These conditions, by definition, apply only to the therapeutic relationship. The three CORE CONDITIONS are not merely a summary but are the qualities of relationship which can be attributed to any relationship.

**SPONTANEITY** See above REFLEXIVITY.

**SURPLUS OF MEANING** In the work of Paul Ricoeur, the idea that because a METAPHOR is inexhaustible for meaning—we can always find more—then every METAPHOR contains a surplus of meaning in which is vested its EXISTENTIAL significance.

**SYMBOLISATION** The process whereby material that has been suppressed, denied to awareness, is moved back into awareness. In other words, the mind develops symbols which represent experience, where such symbols did not previously exist.

TRANSACTIONS In TA, any exchange between two or more people. A transaction can be a single comment in each direction, or it can be judged to persist for a lot longer. Transactions are either ways of communicating information or they are, in Berne's terminology, 'gamey': they are based on an ulterior motive to gain some psychological advantage or defer some threat, relatively independently of the literal meaning of the exchange.

TRANSFERENCE The habit of transferring onto current relationships some or all of the qualities of significant past relationships. For Freud, this had marked therapeutic significance. However, it does exist as an everyday phenomenon. For instance, I notice that when I walk into a room full of strangers I will look for someone who *reminds* me of a familiar person. This then provides a source of vague comfort under stressful circumstances.

TRIMESTER A useful but rather formal term for a three-month period of time. It is particularly used to refer to the stages of foetal development in pregnancy. Melanie Klein extended this to cover the two three-month periods of infancy immediately after birth.

WISCONSIN PROJECT A very large-scale project conducted by Rogers and many others at the University of Wisconsin between 1957 and 1963 in working with people with schizophrenia. The outcome was disappointing not least because the research design was flawed. (See, Barrett-Lennard, 1998: 68–9, 267–70, Kirschenbaum, in press)

# REFERENCES


Adorno, T (2003) *The Jargon of Authenticity*. London: Routledge.

Austin, JL (1961) *How to Do Things with Words*. Oxford: Oxford University Press.

Barrett-Lennard, G (1998) *Carl Rogers' Helping System*. London: Sage.

Berne, E (1964/1968) *Games People Play: The psychology of human relationships*. Harmondsworth: Penguin.

Berne, E (1966) *Principles of Group Treatment*. New York: Grove Press.

Bohart, AC & Tallman, K (1999) *How Clients Make Therapy Work: The process of active self-healing*. Washington, DC: American Psychological Association Books.

Bozarth, J (1998) *Person-Centred Therapy: A revolutionary paradigm*. Ross-on-Wye: PCCS Books.

Brazier, D (1993) The necessary condition is love: Going beyond self in the person-centred approach. In D Brazier (ed) *Beyond Carl Rogers*. London: Constable, pp. 72–91.

Buber, M (1958) *I and Thou*. Edinburgh: T and T Clark.

Campling, M (2006) A DIY cure for anorexia. *Therapy Today 17* (5), 30–2.

Chazan, R (2001) *The Group as Therapist*. London: Jessica Kingsley Publishers.

Clarkson, P (1992) *Transactional Analysis Psychotherapy: An integrated approach*. London: Routledge.

Cohn, HW (1997) *Existential Thought and Therapeutic Practice: An introduction to existential psychotherapy*. London: Sage.

Cooper, D (1990) *Existentialism*. Oxford: Blackwell.

Cooper, M (2003) *Existential Therapies*. London: Sage.

Corey, G (2000) *The Art of Integrative Counseling*. Belmont, CA: Thomson Wadsworth.

Cully, S (2004) *Integrative Counselling Skills in Action*. London: Sage.

Edelman, G (1992) *Bright Air, Brilliant Fire: On the matter of the mind*. London: Allen Lane.

Ellingham, I (2005) Transference, trashed and transcended. *Person-Centred Quarterly*, February 2005, 6–9.

Frankl, V (2004) *Man's Search for Meaning*. London: Rider & Co.

Gendlin, E (1962/1997) *Experiencing and the Creation of Meaning: A philosophical and psychological approach to the subjective*. Evanston, IL: Northwestern University Press.

Gendlin, E (1980) *Focusing*. London: Bantam.

Gibran, K (1926/1964) *The Prophet*. London: Heinemann.

Grant, B (1990/2002) Principled and instrumental nondirectiveness in person-centered and client-centered therapy. *Person-Centered Review,*

5 (1), 77– 88. Reprinted in D Cain (ed) (2002) *Classics in the Person-Centered Approach*. Ross-on-Wye: PCCS Books, pp. 371–6.

Gray, J (2004) *Consciousness: Creeping up on the hard problem*. Oxford: Oxford University Press.

Greenberg, LS, Rice LN & Elliott, R (1993) *Facilitating Emotional Change: The moment-by-moment process*. New York: The Guilford Press.

Harris, JB (2003) *Gestalt: A new idiosyncratic introduction*. Manchester: Manchester Gestalt Centre.

Harris, TA (1970/1973) *I'm OK—You're OK*. London: Pan.

Hobson, RF (1985) *Forms of Feeling: The heart of psychotherapy*. London: Tavistock.

Kirschenbaum, H & Henderson, VL (eds) (1990a) Martin Buber In *Carl Rogers: Dialogues*. London: Constable, pp. 41–63.

Kirschenbaum, H & Henderson, VL (eds:) (1990b) Paul Tillich. In *Carl Rogers: Dialogues*. London: Constable, pp. 64–78.

Kirschenbaum, H (in press) *The Life and Work of Carl Rogers*. Ross-on-Wye: PCCS Books.

Levinas, E (1969) *Totality and Infinity: An essay on exteriority* (Trans A Lingis). Pittsburgh, PA: Duquesne University Press.

McLeod, J (1994) *Doing Counselling Research*. London: Sage.

Macquarrie, J (1972/1991) *Existentialism*. Harmondsworth: Penguin/Pelican.

Mearns, D (1994) *Developing Person-Centred Counselling*. London: Sage.

Mearns, D & Cooper, M (2005) *Working at Relational Depth in Counselling and Psychotherapy*. London: Sage.

Mearns, D & Thorne, B (1988/1999) *Person-Centred Counselling in Action*. London: Sage.

Mearns, D & Thorne, B (2000) *Person-Centred Therapy Today: New frontiers in theory and practice*. London: Sage.

Merry, T (2004) Classical client-centred therapy. In P Sanders (ed) *The Tribes of the Person-Centred Nation: An introduction to the schools of therapy related to the person-centred approach.*. Ross-on-Wye: PCCS Books, pp. 21–44.

Nagel, T (1979) What is it like to be a Bat? In T Nagel (1979) *Mortal Questions*. Cambridge: Cambridge University Press, pp. 165–80.

Norcross, JC & Arkowitz, H (1992) The evolution and current status of psychotherapy integration. In W Dryden (ed) *Integrative and Eclectic Therapy: A handbook*. Buckingham: Open University Press, pp. 1–40.

O'Brien, M (2000) *Integrative Therapy: A practitioner's guide*. London: Sage.

Perls, F, Hefferline, RF & Goodman P (1951/1973) *Gestalt Therapy: Excitement and growth in the human personality*. Harmondsworth: Penguin.

Proctor, G, Cooper, M, Sanders, P & Malcolm, B (eds) (2006) *Politicizing the Person-Centred Approach: An agenda for social change.* Ross-on-Wye: PCCS Books.

Prouty, G, Van Werde, D & Pörtner, M (2002) *Pre-Therapy: Reaching contact-impaired clients*. Ross-on-Wye: PCCS Books.

Rennie, DL (1998) *Person-Centred Counselling: An experiential approach.* London: Sage.

Rennie, DL (2006) Radical reflexivity: Rationale for an experiential person-centered approach to counseling and psychotherapy. *Person-Centered and Experiential Psychotherapies 5* (2), 114–26.

Ricoeur, P (1975/1986). *The Rule of Metaphor: Multi-disciplinary studies of the creation of meaning in language.* London: Routledge.

Rogers, CR (1951) *Client-Centered Therapy*. London: Constable.

Rogers, CR (1955) Persons or science: A philosophical question. *American Psychologist 10* (7), 267–78. Also in CR Rogers *On Becoming a Person: A therapist's view of psychotherapy.* London: Constable, pp.199–224.

Rogers, CR (1957) The necessary and sufficient conditions of therapeutic personality change. *Journal of Consulting Psychology 21* (2), 95–103.

Rogers, CR (1959) A theory of therapy, personality and interpersonal relationships, as developed in the client-centered framework. In S Koch (ed) *Psychology, A Study of Science: 3. Formulations of the person and the social context*. New York: McGraw-Hill, pp. 184–256.

Rogers, CR (1961/1967a) A process conception of psychotherapy. In CR Rogers *On Becoming a Person: A therapist's view of psychotherapy.* London: Constable, pp. 125–59.

Rogers, CR (1961/1967b) To be that self which one truly is: A therapist's view of personal goals. In CR Rogers *On Becoming a Person: A therapist's view of psychotherapy*. London: Constable, pp. 163–82.

Rogers, CR (1963) The actualizing tendency in relation to 'motives' and to consciousness. In MR Jones (ed) *Nebraska Symposium on Motivation.* Lincoln, NB: University of Nebraska Press, pp. 1–24.

Rogers, CR (1986) Reflection of feelings. *Person-Centered Review 1* (4), 375–77.

Rowan, J (1990) *Subpersonalities: The people inside us*. London: Routledge.

Sanders, P (ed) (2004) *The Tribes of the Person-Centred Nation: An introduction to the schools of therapy related to the person-centred approach.* Ross-on-Wye: PCCS Books.

Sanders, P (2005) Principled and strategic opposition to the medicalisation of distress and all of its apparatus. In S Joseph & R Worsley (eds) *Person-Centred Psychopathology: A positive psychology of mental health*. Ross-on-Wye: PCCS Books, pp. 21–42.

Sanders, P (2006) *The Person-Centred Counselling Primer*. Ross-on-Wye: PCCS Books.

Sanders, P (in press) The 'family' of person-centered and experiential therapies. In M Cooper, M O'Hara, PF Schmid & G Wyatt (eds) *The*

*Handbook of Person-Centred Therapy*. Basingstoke: Palgrave.

Schmid, PF (1998) Face-to-Face—the art of encounter. In B Thorne & E Lambers (eds) *Person-Centred Therapy: A European perspective*. London: Sage, pp. 74–90.

Schmid, PF (2005) Authenticity and alienation: Towards an understanding of the person beyond the categories of order and disorder. In S Joseph and R Worsley (eds) *Person-Centred Psychopathology: A positive psychology of mental health*. Ross-on-Wye: PCCS Books, pp. 75–90.

Sills, C, Fish, S & Lapworth, P (1995) *Gestalt Counselling*. Bicester: Winslow Press.

Sommerbeck, L (2005) The complementarity between client-centred therapy and psychiatry: The theory and the practice. In S Joseph and R Worsley (eds) *Person-Centred Psychopathology: A positive psychology of mental health*. Ross-on-Wye: PCCS Books, pp. 110–27.

Spinelli, E (1989) *The Interpreted World: Introduction to phenomenological psychology*. London: Sage.

Stewart, I & Joines, V (1987) *TA Today: A new introduction to Transactional Analysis*. Nottingham: Lifespace.

Tillich, P (1952/1980) *The Courage to Be*. New Haven: Yale University Press.

Thomas, RS (1992) *Mass for Hard Times*. Newcastle-upon-Tyne: Bloodaxe.

Thorne, B (1992) *Carl Rogers*. London: Sage.

Tudor, K & Worrall, M (2004) *Freedom to Practise: Person-centred approaches to supervision*. Ross-on-Wye: PCCS Books.

Tudor, K & Worrall, M (2006) *Person-Centred Therapy: A clinical Philosophy*. London: Routledge.

Villas-Boas Bowen, M (1996) The myth of nondirectiveness: The case of Jill. In BA Farber, DC Brink & PM Raskin (eds) *The Psychotherapy of Carl Rogers: Cases and commentary*. New York: The Guilford Press, pp. 84–94.

Warner, M (2000a) One nation, many tribes. *Person-Centered Journal, 7* (1), 28–39.

Warner, M (2000b) Person-centred therapy at the difficult edge. In D Mearns & B Thorne *Person-Centred Therapy Today: New frontiers in theory and practice*. London: Sage.

Worsley, R (2002) *Process Work in Person-Centred Therapy: Phenomenological and existential perspectives*. Basingstoke: Palgrave.

Worsley, R (2003) Small is beautiful: Small-scale phenomenological research for counsellor self-development. *Person-Centered and Experiential Psychotherapies*, *2* (2), 121–32.

Worsley, R (2004) Integrating with integrity. In P Sanders (ed) *The Tribes of the Person-Centred Nation: An introduction to the schools of therapy related to the person-centred approach*. Ross-on-Wye: PCCS Books, pp.125–47.

Worsley, R (2005) What Would Carl Say? *Therapy Today, 6* (8), October 2005. Rugby: BACP.

Worsley, R & Joseph, S (eds) (2007) *Person-Centred Practice: Case studies in positive psychology.* Ross-on-Wye: PCCS Books.

Yalom, ID (1980) *Existential Psychotherapy*. New York: Basic Books.

Yalom, ID (2001) *The Gift of Therapy: Reflections on being a therapist.* London: Piatkus.

Yontef, GM & Simkin, JF (1989) Gestalt therapy. In R Corsini & D Wedding (eds) *Current Psychotherapies*, 4th edn. Itasca, IL: FE Peacock Inc, pp. 25–35.

# INDEX


acceptance 19, 84
ACTUALISING TENDENCY 10, 12, 21–3, 27, 29, 32, 34, 39, 59, 77, 80, 106
Adorno, T 65, 114
Adult 41–7, 49, 85, 108
ANGST 68, 70, 106
anorexia nervosa 38, 85–6
Arkowitz, H 8, 9, 115
arousal 55
Association for the Development of the Person-Centered Approach (ADPCA) 103
Austin, JL 73, 114
authenticity 65, 67–8
avoidance 55
awareness 12, 33, 36, 38, 40, 52–8, 60, 64, 77, 80, 84, 87, 94–7
  embodied 52–5, 57, 59
  existential 70
  self (see 'self awareness')

bad faith 67
Bandura, A 21
Barrett-Lennard, G 113, 114
BEHAVIOURISM 21, 106
Berne, E 41, 42, 45, 105, 114
BLANK SCREEN 95, 106
Bohart, AC 11, 114
Bozarth, J 27, 105, 109, 110, 114
Brazier, D 88, 114
British Association for the Person-Centred Approach (BAPCA) 103
Buber M 62, 70, 71, 72, 86, 101, 105, 114

Campling, M 38, 114
Chazan, R 39, 114
Child 41–9, 108
Clarkson, P 41, 114
CLASSICAL CLIENT-CENTRED THERAPY 6, 9, 14, 11, 21–2, 64, 81, 106
COGNITIVE-BEHAVIOURAL (THERAPY) 14, 21, 106
Cohn, HW 105, 114
completion 55
CONDITIONS OF WORTH 7, 10, 32–4, 41, 44, 47, 52, 99, 106, 110, 111
  INTROJECTED 97
CONFIGURATIONS OF SELF 17, 31, 32, 33, 36, 37, 40, 42, 47, 78, 81, 96–7, 99
CONGRUENT/CONGRUENCE 8, 11, 19–20, 32, 34–5, 37–8, 40, 48, 52, 67, 79–80, 82, 96, 106, 107, 110
CONSCIOUSNESS 31, 36, 107
CONTACT 107
Cooper, D 105, 114
Cooper, M 62, 67, 105, 114, 115
CORE CONDITIONS 22, 30, 33, 37, 40, 66, 85, 107, 112
Corey, G 8, 114
Cully, S 8, 114

defining counselling 1
depression 2, 23, 34–5, 38, 56, 59, 62, 68–9, 75, 80, 82, 100
Descartes, R 31, 107
diagnosis 2, 11, 21, 65, 86, 108, 110
dialectical process 32
DIALOGIC/DIALOGICAL 38, 61, 107
DIALOGUE 7, 11–13, 16–17, 20, 33, 36, 43, 61, 63, 65–7, 69, 71, 73, 84, 89, 91–2, 97–9, 107
directivity (see also 'non-directivity') 23–6, 40, 60, 66, 76–7, 80–1

disease 11, 38
dissociative identity disorder 33
distress 1–5, 7, 9, 38, 53, 107, 110
dying (see also 'mortality') 15, 93, 101
DYSFUNCTION 10, 40, 58, 70, 107, 109, 110
eating disorders (see also 'anorexia nervosa') 85–6
ECLECTIC/ECLECTICISM 8–11, 21, 27, 108, 110
Edelman, G 36, 114
Ego 32
EGO-STATE 41–3, 108
Ellingham, I 50, 114
Embleton Tudor, L 104
EMBODIED awareness 52–60
empathy/empathic 6, 28, 40, 47–8, 59, 74, 81–2, 84, 89, 91, 107
emptiness 70
empty chair 52
encounter 22, 61–3, 65, 66, 73, 92, 96, 102, 108
EXISTENTIAL 16, 62, 66–70, 94–5, 106
  anxiety 56, 68
  encounter 73
  intervention 66
  knowledge 62, 64–5
  moment 93
  philosophy 15, 16, 66, 68, 106
  self 61
  therapy 67–8
EXISTENTIALISM 66–70
EXPERIENTIAL 8, 108, 112
  therapists 24

fantasies 55
fate 69
felt-sense 26
FIGURE 55–7
  AND GROUND 53, 108
Fish, S 54, 117
fluency 94, 101
FOCUSING 8, 76, 81, 108
FRAGILE PROCESS 22, 108
FRAME OF REFERENCE 17, 37, 43–4, 59, 77–81, 108–9
Frankl, V 27, 105, 114
Freud, S 32, 113
FULLY FUNCTIONING 95

GAME/s 44–6, 109
Gendlin, E 54, 59, 60, 80, 108, 114
GESTALT 52–3, 108–9
  cycle of awareness 87
  cycle of experience 55
  psychology 53
  therapist 27, 55
  therapy 13, 15–16, 25, 53–4, 60, 80, 109
Gibran, K 19, 114
GOOD LIFE, the 67, 109
Grant, B 19, 24, 114
Gray, J 36, 115
Greenberg, LS 52, 54, 115
groups 39–41

Harris, JB 54, 115
Harris, TA 41, 105, 115
Hefferline, RF 52, 54, 57, 58, 115
Henderson, VL 66, 98, 115
Hobson, RF 85, 91, 95, 115
HOLISM 11, 23, 29, 109
HORIZONTALISATION 25, 109
humanness 71

I–Thou 63, 71–2, 86, 91, 107
Id 32
IDIOSYNCRATIC 6, 13, 16, 28, 29, 62, 64, 82, 109
incongruence (see also 'congruence') 11, 32—5, 37–8, 52, 97, 106, 107, 110
information 110, 113
initiation 55
inner zone 54, 58
interpretation 10, 37, 50, 58, 84
INTROJECT/INTROJECTION 32, 44, 55, 97–8, 106, 110–11

intuit/intuition 7, 28, 31, 53, 71–2, 86
Joines, V 42, 105, 117
Joseph, S 69, 104, 118
Keemar, K 104
Kirschenbaum, H 66, 98, 115

levels of intervention 17
Levinas, E 62, 72, 115
LOCUS OF EVALUATION 25, 110

Macquarrie, J 66, 67, 105, 115
McLeod, J 83, 115
Mearns, D 31, 32, 33, 34, 35, 37, 39, 42, 59, 61, 62, 85, 96, 99, 104, 115
MEDICAL MODEL 18, 100, 110
Merry, T 104, 115
METAPHOR 37, 39, 81–2, 92, 94–5, 99, 110, 113
middle zone 54
mortality (see also 'dying') 68, 70, 92–4

Nagel, T 72, 115
narrow ridge 101–2
Nazi concentration camp 27
NECESSARY AND SUFFICIENT CONDITIONS (see also 'SIX CONDITIONS') 26–7, 110
NINETEEN PROPOSITIONS 31, 94, 111
NON-DIRECTIVE/NESS 12, 19, 24–6, 60, 81, 111
- instrumental 24–6
- principled 23–6, 29, 60
- therapy 111

Norcross, JC 8, 9, 115

O'Brien, M 8, 115
O'Leary, C 29
ontology/ontological 111
organism 21–2, 32, 52, 54, 57, 109, 111
ORGANISMIC VALUING PROCESS 32, 34–5, 67, 96, 98, 107, 110–11
Other 72–3
Otherness 72
outer zone 54
Parent-Adult-Child (PAC) 41–51
Parent 41, 44
Perls, F 27, 52, 54, 55, 56, 57, 58, 59, 60, 110, 115
Person-Centered and Experiential Psychotherapies (PCEP) 103
person-centred integration 8
personal growth 4
PHENOMENOLOGY/ICAL 13, 16, 41–4, 47, 52, 58, 76, 91, 109, 111
PLATONIC THOUGHT 31, 111
practitioner research 83–90
PRE-THERAPY 111
PRIMARY PREVENTION RESEARCH 4
PROCESS DIRECTION 112
Proctor, G 49, 66, 115
profession 1
PROTOCOL 27, 41, 112
Prouty, G, 116
PSYCHODYNAMIC/APPROACH 10, 13–14, 16, 84, 112
PSYCHOTIC 63, 111, 112

reassurance 19, 48
reductionism 109
reflection of feelings 6, 28, 61
REFLECTIVE PRACTICE 19, 47, 112
REFLEXIVE/REFLEXIVITY 36, 55, 94, 107, 112
Rennie, DL 24, 36, 81, 116
REPRESSION 112
research 83–90
Rice LN 54, 115
Ricoeur, P 99, 116
risk 13, 19–20, 37, 48, 50, 59, 63, 76, 79, 80
Rogers, CR 6, 11, 13, 21, 22, 26, 27, 28, 31, 36, 52, 54, 55, 56, 63, 66, 67, 84, 96, 98, 107, 110, 111, 112, 113, 116
Rowan, J 33, 36, 116

safety 6, 17, 20, 25, 85
Sanders, P 6, 8, 12, 13, 26, 38, 41, 64, 81, 104, 105, 116
satisfaction 55
Schmid, P 22, 61, 62, 63, 64, 65, 66, 71, 107, 117
self 12, 14, 16–7, 22, 31–40, 47, 57, 61, 91–102
  awareness 2, 58, 64, 66, 86, 112
  concept 32, 34, 35, 38, 106, 108, 111, 112
  confidence 3, 66, 69, 70
  configurations (see 'configurations of self')
  realisation 66
  structure 10, 94, 95, 96, 98, 107, 108, 112
sex 2, 45
Sills, C 54, 105, 117
Simkin, JF 54, 118
six conditions 28, 29, 84, 110
SIX CONDITIONS/of therapy (see also 'necessary and sufficient conditions') 11, 26, 28–9, 84, 107, 110–11
Sommerbeck, L 14, 117
Spinelli, E 25, 117
SPONTANEITY 55, 112
Stevens, JO 105
Stewart, I 42, 105, 117
subpersonalities (see also 'configurations of self') 33, 96
Superego 32
supervision 20, 50, 84, 86, 96
SURPLUS OF MEANING 94, 99, 113
SYMBOLISATION 36, 113

Tallman, K 11, 114
technique 11, 24, 26, 28
tenderness 48, 77, 89
Thomas, RS 100, 101, 117
Thorne, B 31, 33, 35, 39, 48, 61, 85, 89, 96, 97, 115, 117
Thou–I relationship 64
threat 50, 68, 94, 97, 113
Tillich, P 66, 69, 70, 98, 105, 117
Tolan, J 104
Transactional Analysis (TA) 16, 41–50, 62, 85, 108–9, 113
TRANSFERENCE 75, 76, 78, 81, 82, 106, 113
transparency 87, 89
TRIMESTER 113
Tudor, K 20, 104, 105, 117

unconditional positive regard (UPR) 86, 96, 107
unconscious 10, 36, 45, 80, 93, 107, 112

Van Werde, D 116
Villas-Boas Bowen, M 20, 22, 117

Warner, M 17, 108, 117
Wilkins, P 104
WISCONSIN PROJECT 63, 113
World Association for Person-Centered and Experiential Psychotherapies 103
Worrall, M 105, 117
Worsley, R 13, 24, 54, 55, 69, 86, 104, 105, 117
Wyatt, G 104, 105

Yalom, ID 6, 61, 68, 105, 118
Yontef, GM 54, 118

Zeigarnik 53, 55
  effect 55
Zinker, J 105

*The Primers in Counselling Series* **by PCCS Books**

This best-selling series offers comprehensive descriptions of key counselling approaches and contexts in the 21st century. Accessible and concise, they are ideal for students seeking a theory bridge between introductory, intermediate and diploma courses or for comparative essays and integrative theory assignments.

The other primers in the series are:

***The Focusing-Oriented Counselling Primer*** (2nd edition) – Campbell Purton pbk 9781915220004 – epub 9781915220011

***The Rational Emotive Behaviour Therapy Primer*** – Windy Dryden pbk 9781910919965 – epub 9781910919972

***The Pluralistic Therapy Primer*** – Kate Smith and Ani de la Prida pbk 9781910919866 – epub 9781910919873

***The Single-Session Counselling Primer*** – Windy Dryden pbk 9781910919569 – epub 9781910919583

***The Existential Counselling Primer*** (2nd edition) – Mick Cooper pbk 9781910919750 – epub 9781910919767

***The Person-Centred Counselling Primer*** – Pete Sanders pbk 9781898059806 – epub 9781906254841

***The Cognitive Behaviour Therapy Primer*** (2nd edition) – Rhena Branch, Jodie Paget & Windy Dryden
pbk 9781910919989 – epub 9781910919996

***The Experiential Counselling Primer*** – Nick Baker
pbk 9781898059837

***The Contact Work Primer: Introduction to pre-therapy*** – edited by Pete Sanders: pbk 9781898059844

***The Psychodynamic Counselling Primer*** – Mavis Klein
pbk 9781898059851 – epub 9781906254896

**Discounted prices and free UK P&P – www.pccs-books.co.uk**